Reparations

A PLAN FOR CHURCHES

Reparations

A PLAN FOR CHURCHES

PETER JARRETT-SCHELL

Foreword by Stephanie Spellers

 Church Publishing
NEW YORK

Unless otherwise noted, the Scripture quotations are from the New Revised Standard Version Bible, copyright © 1989 National Council of the Churches of Christ in the United States of America. Used by permission. All rights reserved worldwide.

Church Publishing
19 East 34th Street
New York, NY 10016

Cover design by Joseph Piliero

Library of Congress Cataloging-in-Publication Data
Names: Jarrett-Schell, Peter, author.
Title: Reparations : a plan for churches / Peter Jarrett-Schell.
Description: New York, NY : Church Publishing, [2022]
Identifiers: LCCN 2022051739 (print) | LCCN 2022051740 (ebook) | ISBN
    9781640656093 (paperback) | ISBN 9781640656109 (ebook)
Subjects: LCSH: United States—Race relations. | African
    Americans—Reparations. | Race relations—Religious
    aspects—Christianity.
Classification: LCC E185.89.R45 J37 2022 (print) | LCC E185.89.R45
    (ebook) | DDC 305.896/073—dc23/eng/20221129
LC record available at https://lccn.loc.gov/2022051739
LC ebook record available at https://lccn.loc.gov/2022051740

For Joshua D'Miguel, who deserved better.
Some harms can never be repaired.

Contents

Foreword

I was a late adopter on reparations. For years, I aligned with pragmatic leaders like President Barack Obama who said reparations are "justified" but that during his presidency "the politics of white resistance and resentment" made it "politically not only a nonstarter but potentially counterproductive."[1]

Our camp wondered what money alone could accomplish in the face of such abject, multi-generational trauma and a system of racism that touches and corrodes every facet of American life. We worried that reparations would be a dangerous panacea, one that would placate white folks who desperately want to believe you can write a check and be done with racism.

We were also deeply suspicious of hush money, as in, if People of Color accept this money, we must be silent (or white folk could officially *not* listen if we did cry out). And deep down, I shared Obama's concern that the very word "reparations" could set off a backlash that ignites more trouble than it could ever heal.

And so we pragmatists stood back. Then a funny, holy thing happened. People took seriously the fact that other nations had issued apologies and reparations, and the sky did not fall. In fact, these very United States provided reparations in the form of payments to Japanese people held in World War II internment camps.

In 2021, Representative Sheila Jackson reintroduced HR 40—thirty years after Representative John Conyers first introduced the bill that would create a commission to study

---

1. "Race in the United States," episode 2 of "Renegades: Born in the USA" podcast featuring Barack Obama and Bruce Springsteen. February 2021. https://open.spotify .com/show/42xagX CUDsFO6a0lcHoTlv. Sourced on November 3, 2022.

reparations and recommend concrete steps forward. This time, nearly 200 representatives signed on as co-sponsors, with 22 senators supporting the cognate bill Cory Booker brought to the Senate chamber. Institutions across the land are tumbling forth to proclaim their commitment to reparations.

Something has changed in America. Something has also shifted in our Episcopal church. Since 2017, we have been engaged in a churchwide, lifelong journey toward racial healing, justice and reconciliation. Known as Becoming Beloved Community, this journey is like the spiritual practice of walking a labyrinth. As you traverse the sections or quadrants, you move through different phases and practices, sometimes retracing steps through territory you thought you knew, eventually coming to the center only to find you will now voyage back out the way you came.

Moving through these quadrants, we *tell the truth* about our churches and race: things done and left undone, things erased and people stolen. We name and *proclaim God's dream for beloved community*, the vision that compels us to keep moving through the muck and mire, the hope that will not let us go. We train, learn, and *practice the healing, reconciling way of Jesus*, knowing our ways are not his ways … but they could be. And sooner or later, we roll up our sleeves and work to *repair the breach*, addressing racism's impact on institutions, communities, and society, so they function and flourish in the just way that God intends.

We've been talking "repair" like this for a long time, but until more recently, we haven't as a whole church been seriously talking "reparations." It has taken time to wrap our lips and minds around the word. We had to become braver and more imaginative to embrace this concept, along with similarly taboo terms like "white supremacy" and "anti-Black." Certainly the brutal, public murders of George Floyd and other Black people unlocked something. We have collectively witnessed the depths of American depravity and understand that, if we want to heal and transform this nation and all her people, every option has to be on the table.

It took me a while, but I am deeply grateful that Jarrett-Schell and the leaders assembled in this book have called upon the church to not only embrace reparations but to lead on it. Christians need only to listen to our sacred scriptures and look to our Savior if we want to understand the priority of reparations. Jesus regularly issued the invitation to sacrifice and self-emptying on the journey toward new life. Especially when he encountered people with privilege, he was clear on the path to salvation: change your ways, relinquish your hold on privilege, admit what you have received at the expense of others, and make amends to those who have been hurt by the very systems designed to benefit you. Then you will know eternal life.

The gospels show us two radically different responses to Jesus's invitation. There is the rich young man in Matthew 19. He came asking about eternal life, and Jesus told him to sell his possessions and give the proceeds to the poor. In essence, he broke the hard news: you got it at their expense; now you've got to heal what's been broken. Matthew says the rich young man hung his head and walked away. You will notice that Jesus does not reassure him or take back the challenge. Jesus spoke a true word to his brother in love, and then he let the young man walk, pray and re-examine his life in light of this troubling but good news. We do not actually know what he chose in the end. But we know Jesus held out a path that led through truth and sacrifice, into freedom and abundant life.

In Luke 19, Jesus makes a similar offer to Zacchaeus, the chief tax collector whose schemes wounded and defrauded people at the bottom. Zacchaeus might not have built that system, and he might not have fully grasped his own participation, but he certainly benefited from it. Jesus notices Zacchaeus up high (in a tree!) and says, "Come down from there. I want to go to your house." Jesus draws near Zacchaeus and offers him mercy, grace and hard truth. Zacchaeus responds with miraculous enthusiasm, confessing what he has done wrong and then promising to make it right. He says: "Here and now, I'm giving half of what I own to the poor, and if I have cheated anybody, I will pay back four times what I received."

Jesus held out his hand. Zacchaeus took it. That act of vulnerability and surrender changed everything. A similar alchemy could happen for white people and institutions via reparations.

So many followers of Jesus have already begun this journey, and they now comprise a dedicated community who can guide all of us to take risks, investigate our histories, and make genuine headway around reparations in the church. The list gets longer every few months: dioceses like those in New York, Maryland, Washington, Virginia, Texas, and Massachusetts; congregations like Memorial Church in Baltimore; schools like Virginia Theological Seminary. Together they stand as compelling witnesses and exhibit a comprehensive way forward.

And so we come to this moment, when you now hold a book titled *Reparations: A Plan for the Church*, written and compiled by a white Episcopal priest and a broader community of people (many of them Black leaders) who have led real efforts toward actual reparations. This book could not have existed 30 years ago or perhaps even three years ago. It is a book for people at all points along the journey, for the skeptical and the imaginative, the practical and the theological, the philosophical, and even the mathematical.

Jarrett-Schell and his colleagues do not advocate for the ministry of check-writing, which is good because reparations is so much more than choosing a number (even a large one) and distributing the proceeds to People of Color (even direct descendants). They understand that reparations demands a reorientation in our relationship with God, our neighbors and our own broken, frightened, yearning selves. It is sacrificial. It is intentional. It is humble and non-controlling. It is other-centered and not self-centric. It is not political. It is all about Jesus and his way of love. As Jarrett-Schell puts it: "Reparations could be part of the slow process of freeing ourselves from the gilded cage of white supremacy that holds us, melting it down, and making of it something new. I want to invite you to consider the process of reparations as a process of grace, relationship, and creativity."

Like the Beloved Community labyrinth, the commitment to reparations moves through several phases. Jarrett-Schell and his partners lay out a six-step plan that I hope every congregation and institution considering reparations will take to heart. According to the leaders he consults, there can be no reparations without first *building relationship* and getting to know the actual community that has been harmed. There should be *truth-finding* and honest, thorough investigation of histories, practices, finances, archives—how else do you know what you're sorry for? Having learned these truths, we can then engage in *truth-telling*, that specific statement of things done and left undone, a confessional practice that should be familiar (if still difficult) for Christians. Liturgy-loving Episcopalians may want to craft a repentance liturgy as step 1, but

Jarrett-Schell and his colleagues rightly advise that *individual and corporate repentance* only makes sense after we have done the painful, humbling work of interior reflection and confession.

Not until step five are we ready to speak meaningfully and realistically of *reparation*. This could be direct financial restitution to people and/or institutions for specific harm. It could also mean white people and institutions finding concrete ways to sacrifice and surrender financial and other resources, and share them so that People of Color can heal and renew our institutions and communities as we see fit. Some have established grant programs. Others are making direct investments in schools, housing, health initiatives or other transformative strategies. As long as white people and institutions aren't pulling the strings and controlling outcomes, and as long as it is intentional and sacrificial, we do not need to be purists about a single form of reparations.

And yes, there is a sixth step—*evaluation*—to ensure we are accountable to the truths and communities with which we started and that the lifelong work indeed continues.

I find such hope and good news in these pages. The truth will not destroy us. Reparations will not destroy us. The only thing the truth destroys is narratives and structures built on lies, none of which should have stood in the first place. Reparations attempts to right those wrongs and resets that balance, so that all might flourish in body, mind, and spirit.

Thanks be to God for Peter Jarrett-Schell and the wise community assembled in this book. Together they help us boldly, faithfully respond to Jesus's invitation to speak the truth, repent, empty, and be humbled, all so that we might fully embrace the lifelong ministry of dismantling racism and becoming one beloved community. However politically inexpedient it might be, I hope we will accept the invitation as Episcopalians and as children of God. This is how we all get free.

Stephanie Spellers
Reverend Canon to the Presiding Bishop for Evangelism,
Reconciliation and Creation Care
Author of *The Church Cracked Open: Disruption,
Decline and New Hope for Beloved Community*
November 2022
Harlem, New York

Preface

I grew up with a mother who loves Shakespeare. I spent more time in the theater, at Shakespeare in the park, or watching movie adaptations of the Bard's work than any other child I knew. I didn't love it. I struggled with the language. My mind would wander, and lose track of the thread, leaving me scrambling to catch up when I drifted back to the scene before me. But, now and again, bits and fragments would stick with me, lodged in my memory for years to come. As an adult, I'm often surprised at the odd ways these fragments float to the surface, nudging and directing my thinking.

Which is a roundabout way of explaining the absurd fact that, when I think of racial justice and what it requires, I see the face, and hear the voice, of British actor, Sir Derek Jacobi, playing Claudius in Kenneth Branagh's film adaptation of *Hamlet*. There's a moment when he sits in a confessional, and prays, or tries to pray, for absolution, longing to be forgiven for the murder of his brother, and the theft of the throne:

> But, O, what form of prayer can serve my turn? 'Forgive me my foul murder'?
>
> That cannot be; since I am still possess'd of those effects for which I did the murder,
>
> My crown, mine own ambition and my queen. May one be pardon'd and retain the offence?
>
> In the corrupted currents of this world Offence's gilded hand may shove by justice,
>
> And oft 'tis seen the wicked prize itself buys out the law: but 'tis not so above;
>
> There is no shuffling.

And look, I'm not trying to promote Shakespeare as some anti-racist oracle. Dr. Ayanna Thompson has written whole books on how Shakespeare himself helped shape the concepts and categories of our current racial caste system. And yet, in these words he penned for Claudius, he seems to reach out of the past, and lay his finger on the double talk of my own family, the white Church, when it comes to racial justice.

Like Claudius, we (that is, white Christians) see (or at least guess) the violent and brutal history of our church's participation in white supremacy, and the benefit we've received from it. In the back of our minds, we wonder if our hands, also, are thick with Black blood. This may sound melodramatic. But I think it's more true than we like to admit.

We often claim ignorance, or surprise, when the full record of anti-Black racism is laid before us. But I suspect that our immediate defensiveness, the excuses we make when the question comes up, reveal some awareness of the truth. When I follow the tracks of my own mind and history, I know I only get defensive in the face of charges I know to be true, in some fashion. Baseless accusations don't get under my skin. I would guess it's the same for most of us. We aren't as ignorant as we claim. We know the truth, at least in part.

Like Claudius, many of us (again, white Christian) genuinely lament and regret the harm and offense of racism. We long for justice, and genuine reconciliation. We ache to see all God's children free, respected and thriving. We want true relationships across lines of race, uninterrupted by the trauma and distrust left in racism's wake.

But, like Claudius, we still cling to the effects of the crime: the unjust privileges, deference, and wealth that white supremacy delivers to us. This is, in some sense, a private matter, but it's a corporate one as well. My own denomination, the Episcopal

Church has been, and remains, one of the wealthiest-per-capita denominations in this country. That wealth, the wealth of our congregations and dioceses, was gained, in large part, by plunder: the plunder of native lands, the plunder of Black lives. There can be no healing, no genuine way forward while we still clutch these ill-gotten gains.

I'm going to assume that if you picked up a book like this, you are among those who long to see your Black and brown siblings free, respected and thriving. That's a good longing. Those are good, Kin-dom, values.

But we must be honest: in a world where political freedoms, recognition, representation, and even health outcomes are all deeply dependent on the wealth one possesses, there is no path from where we now stand to the Kin-dom of God that doesn't pass through reparation for the extraordinary wealth stolen from our Black and brown siblings.

Any project of racial justice we undertake that does not include restitution and reparation is necessarily incomplete and insincere. There's a reason Jesus teaches us: "where your treasure is, there your heart will be also." We put our wealth toward things that matter to us. We become personally invested in the places where we've put money. Wealth both follows, and leads, our hearts.

Until we put our money where our mouth is, our Black and brown siblings will likely continue to regard our anti-racist collaborations (whatever they may be) with justified skepticism. If our hope is racial reconciliation, we will need to let go of the unjust riches we hold. I think, on some level, we understand that. But still we clutch.

And I get it. Maybe we're afraid that paying the debt will leave us destitute and vulnerable. Maybe we look at the long trends of decline afflicting our denominations and wonder if, for instance, the Episcopal Church (a still overwhelmingly, though not entirely, white institution) could survive the massive cost of genuine restitution. I share that fear. I make my living in this church. The prospect of its dissolution fills me with uncertainty. And it is true that paying the debt our denomination owes to Black and Indigenous Americans might dissolve the Episcopal Church as we know it.

But I cannot overemphasize the importance of those last four words: "the Episcopal Church *as we know it.*" The Episcopal Church, as we know it, is defined by a long history of entanglement with white supremacy. Even our best, and most loving, moments of anti-racist courage aren't free from this legacy. We can never change that history. But reparations and restitution offer hope, real hope, that we don't have to be shackled to that history forever.

There's another literary fragment from my childhood that sticks with me. Every year, during the season of advent my father would read to us from Dickens's *A Christmas Carol* (yes, I was raised by a pair of literary nerds). At the age of eight, behind my eyelids, I imagined with perfect clarity the awful sight of Jacob Marley and his cohort of ghosts bound and dragged down by their chains of cash boxes and ledgers: the ill-gotten wealth of their history.

This is the story of our church: chained to the wealth of ill-gotten gains that drag us down to perdition (I'll leave to the theologians to decide whether that's a symbolic or literal assessment.) In church growth circles, it's become almost a cliché to note how our real property may be more of an impediment than an asset to our mission. In so many of our congregations our buildings, frequently our greatest single asset, those buildings sitting on stolen Indigenous lands, built in many cases by enslaved Black hands, have become tombs for dying communities.

I feel a dreadful inevitability facing the erosion of the Episcopal Church. It runs parallel to a sense of despair in the face of white supremacy: like there's nothing that could be done about either. But the whole idea of inevitability is one of the lies white supremacy teaches us. When we believe that the sorry state of the world cannot be changed, we lose the fight before it's started.

When asked if there was hope for our future, climate activist Brandon Wu answered, "Hope is a political choice." I would call this the practical application of the admonition we receive from Hebrews: "Faith is the assurance of things hoped for, the conviction of things not seen" (Hebrews 11:1). In the current moment, I believe the Episcopal Church is called upon to make that defiant choice for hope: to believe, and act, with the conviction that the legacy of white supremacy which has defined us is not the end of our story.

Once, I think when I was ten, my parents dragged me off to a Japanese Noh-Theater production of *A Christmas Carol* (again, I was raised by a pair of theater nerds). Beyond the style, the music, and the costumes, what struck me about this production, the great difference between it and the story I knew so well, was its conclusion. In this play, after his conversion, confession and repentance, after he made restitution in monetary terms, Ebeneezer Scrooge met the ghost of Jacob Marley one more time. And then, link by link, cash box by cash box, he freed his old friend from the chains of their shared making.

I wonder: what would happen if we took these congregational tombs we call buildings, and surrendered them to the Black and brown communities to whom, by right, they're owed? Could they become places of resurrection? What would happen if we sold these assets and gave the money, as once Jesus counseled a rich young man, to the very people we have impoverished? What would these Black and brown communities, finally receiving a just recompense so long denied, do with the wealth surrendered to them? Would it go for health care? Education? Housing? Arts? Simple relaxation and joy? All of these: signs of life, signs of resurrection.

And what would happen to the white church communities who chose to surrender the debt at last? What would Jacob Marley do if his chains of ill-gotten gain were broken, and the wealth from which they were forged returned to those from whom it was stolen? I like to think he would dance.

Introduction

Six years ago, Georgetown University acknowledged that in 1838 it sold 272 enslaved people of African descent to prop up its failing finances. The university followed that acknowledgment with a project to make restitution and reparation for the sale.

In the wake of Georgetown's effort, other universities, religious institutions, and municipalities, including four Episcopal dioceses and the Virginia Theological Seminary (VTS), undertook their own reparations initiatives. Last year, congress gave HR 40, *The Commission to Study and Develop Reparation Proposals for African-Americans Act*, its first serious hearing in decades.

The call for reparations, long derided as an unworkable dream of the extreme fringe, has stepped onto the mainstream debate stage, and from there entered into the realm of practice. The Holy Spirit, it seems, is on the move again, leading God's people toward repentance. But, as is so often the case, we find ourselves stumbling along the path.

Despite some admirable successes, each of the initiatives mentioned above have fallen short in varying measures. Our institutions have faltered along the way to repentance. Too often we have become mired in ruts of unambiguously low targets, lapsed promises, and weak accountability.

In the church, the principal culprit of these shortcomings has been a failure of nerve among white Christians. We have flinched from squarely facing the truth of our participation in anti-Black racism. We have turned aside when the road toward restitution seemed overly long, or the cost too high. We have been unwilling to truly humble ourselves, and let the Black community itself teach us what reparations mean. The cost of these failures is measured in disappointment, frustration, and broken trust, for everyone involved. These failings have described us as white Christians.

But they don't have to define us. We can still choose to face the whole truth, to walk the road of restitution from beginning to end, to pay the full price, to learn from the communities we have wronged. We can open our imaginations to the wider creative possibilities of restitution that God lays before us. We can still choose redemption. Nothing less than the soul and integrity of the Episcopal Church is at stake.

The book you're about to read aims to provide spiritual resources and practical tools for individual white Christians as well as predominantly white congregations, dioceses, and other religious institutions who are poised to seize this crucial moment.

Already public ardor for reparations has begun to cool. But it isn't cold yet. Now is the time for our communities to kindle the embers of the Holy Spirit, and carry them forward along the path toward repentance, reparation, and reconciliation.

This book is an argument in favor of a bold risk: that the Episcopal Church (and any other white denominations who might be reading over our shoulders) should transfer 14.7% of their total assets (including real estate) to local Black- and brown-led organizations working for economic empowerment in their communities.

This debt is owed for the benefit the church has received from four hundred years of participation in anti-Black racism. It should be paid, not only as a matter of moral imperative, but also for its potential to help break the Episcopal Church from the gilded shackles of white supremacy that have defined our history. Until reparations are paid, they will define our future as well.

I want to think together about what that process might look like, about how you can take up the work in your local community, and about the surprising, life-filled possibilities we might encounter along the way.

Taking the ongoing, and still-developing, efforts of the Reparations Task Force of the Episcopal Diocese of Washington (EDOW) as a working example, I want to lay out stages of a potential process toward reparations. I'm going to highlight the many pitfalls and opportunities along the way. Congregations and dioceses can use these stages as a template for their own journeys.

I won't, and can't, claim the authority of an expert trail guide. But I can offer the simple solidarity of a fellow traveler walking a difficult road. Don't fret though. We'll have some very capable guides to lead the way.

After doing a bit of preparatory work, stretching our imaginations for what follows, we'll get to the core of the book, a basic framework for a six-stage process toward making reparation. This process has been shaped through interviews with nine seasoned veterans working in the field of racial justice and reparations. They'll share with us their insight, unique perspectives and wisdom, helping us find a way forward along a road that has not yet been charted.

Six of these nine trail guides are Black. This is appropriate and essential. Those who know the impact of anti-Black racism directly, in their own lives, are the ones most competent and capable of helping us find the way past it. Having said that, I have included three white voices as well. For those of us who are white, finding examples of responsible engagement in this work is important. It gives a means to imagine what our own walk along this path might look like.

This journey called reparations is, without a doubt, a difficult and dangerous proposition, that puts the future of our denomination in question. But we followed a guy who said, "Whoever would save their life will lose it, and those who lose their life for my sake will find it." I think maybe it's time we took him at his word.

1

Dreaming Big Dreams

The Math of Reparations

It can be easy to disengage when we talk about reparations. Maybe, like me, you experience feelings of guilt for what's been done. Maybe you get defensive, as if you're being personally accused. Maybe, faced with the horrors and harms of four hundred years of racist abuse, you despair that there's no way to make it right. Let's take a breath together.

I want you to imagine the joy that tax collector Zacchaeus might have felt as he came down from the tree and freely promised, in as far as he was able, to make right all the wrongs that had enriched him.

We, both Black and white alike, have spent centuries bound to a history of racist oppression. Reparations could be part of the slow process of freeing ourselves from the gilded cage of white supremacy that holds us, melting it down, and making of it something new. I want to invite you to consider the process of reparations as a process of grace, relationship and creativity.

Reparations is a process of grace. We will make mistakes along the way. In my role as Chair of the Reparations Task Force for the EDOW, I have made so many mistakes. I will continue to make more. Mistakes are a given. What matters is trying again and doing better each time.

Reparations is a process borne of relationship. In striving to repair this history of harm, we work alongside the very communities we have wronged. We must let them lead us in how to move toward repair and healing. This relationship can at times be rough and uncomfortable, but it can also be deeply loving, in the truest, most uncompromising sense of the word.

Reparations is a creative process, one of looking at all these unjustly amassed riches, letting go, learning from those directly impacted what could be done, and imagining new possibilities together. And there are so many possibilities.

Without a doubt, reparations is a difficult journey. To date, no one has walked that road to its end. But we must begin somewhere, in spite of our dis-ease. Certainly, there is no way to broach the question of reparations without some degree of pain and discomfort. As we start out on this path, it will be important for us to distinguish between that pain and discomfort that sometimes comes with growth, and the kind of hand-wringing anxiety that so often keeps us stuck where we are. Under the right circumstances, pain and discomfort can be productive. This is not true of anxiety.

If we are to receive the grace, relationality and creativity of reparations work, we must find our way past the anxiety, the what-about-isms and denial that would try to waylay us before we even get started.

In my own life, I've found the best remedy for anxiety is to face our pain and discomfort head on, with all the imagination and vision I can muster. To that end, I want to offer one particular vision of what reparations might look like.

As I offer it, I repeat this disclaimer: it is not for me, or for any white person, to determine the shape and form reparations will take. That wisdom must come from the communities who have been directly harmed by white supremacy. They know, and can teach us, what must be done.

So in that spirit, I offer my own vision not as a prescription, or a specific plan. I offer it as an exercise in opening the horizons of our shared imagination.

There is a great danger when considering any new possibility for the first time, that we set our targets too low, that we let our dreams be stingy. In general, when working for reform and change, we achieve less than we have hoped or aspired. If we start our work with a meager vision, we are setting ourselves up to achieve even less than that: a mere pittance. We must choose to think big so that when we hear challenging visions of reparation from folks with skin in the game (and you will hear them in subsequent chapters) we are prepared to receive, listen and imagine what could be. You can think of this chapter as a warm-up before your real trainers arrive to lead the work out.

I want to suggest that white Americans and predominantly white American institutions (such as the Episcopal Church) could make plausible and substantive restitution to Black Americans for the strictly economic effects of white supremacy by transferring 14.7% of their total assets (including real estate) to Black-led organizations working on economic empowerment in Black communities. No dollar figure could ever make fair recompense for 400 years of brutal oppression, but I think restitution would be a good idea, aiming for specific, measurable goals is also salutary. And white churches should be the ones to go first.

I'm not just pulling this figure out of thin air. I've done some math to get there. Like reparations, math often provokes reflexive anxiety in many people. But, like reparations, math's true character is creative and wondrous.

Some time ago, while having a more or less casual conversation with another white person, the topic of reparations came up. I don't remember exactly how, but I do remember my companion making a comment that I have heard, in one form or another, many times before. In fact I've thought it myself on several occasions.

"I'm not saying reparations aren't justified. I'm just saying they're not feasible."

I've never found a satisfactory response to this idea. But this time, for the first time, rather than frustration, the comment sparked a question for me:

"What might reparations look like, at the ground level, in specific terms?"

I went home, got out a ballpoint pen and an old envelope and tried my hand at an estimate. The result I came to is that white America could make substantive and plausible restitution for the strictly financial impact of white supremacy by transferring 14.7% of total assets to Black America, roughly $14.25 trillion in total. A friend of mine, and a member of the diocese's Reparations Task Force, Caroline Klam, suggested that a good criterion for reparations is: "substantial, doable and a little bit painful." Transferring 14.7% of total white wealth is definitely all three.

As a Christian, and something of a softy in general (not that those things necessarily go together), I admit that my own forlorn hope for the future of this nation is a kind of post-racial utopia: a beloved community sustained across lines of diversity, where we cherish one another's differences, labor together for the common good, and ensure all people have what they need to thrive.

In my imagined future, we have abandoned the fiction of race, while still proudly claiming, knowing and living our distinct cultures, heritages and histories. On Thursdays we probably get together to make s'mores around a campfire, while singing Kum Ba Yah (not forgetting to pass around a collection jar for royalties to the Gullah community that wrote it). It's that kind of place.

I suspect many people could get on board with a vision like that, at least in theory. Unfortunately, there are some logistical hurdles in this plan that we tend to overlook.

Liberal Christians often define this collective utopian objective as "Racial Reconciliation." The ideal is noble, but our push for it may be premature. The fact is, we aren't ready for reconciliation. Not yet. We have work to do first. Promoting racial reconciliation, as a first-order goal is essentially equivalent to throwing a house-warming party for a home that hasn't been built yet.

We can't truly come together as one community while some of us still reap benefits from the sabotage of others. No one could ever gather in a genuine community with their own saboteurs. There is an order to these things, and it can't be circumvented: justice precedes reconciliation. Reconciliation precedes community.

Those first two steps are tough. Racialized sabotage and theft were foundational for our nation. As Ibram X. Kendi observed: it's "Stamped from the Beginning." We can find its traces and ongoing effects in every corner of our lives. Given this pervasive influence, when considered soberly, "Racial Reconciliation" would require an almost-Apocalyptic-level reorganization of society.

That might sound very doom and gloom, but, as a Christian, I uphold an Apocalyptic faith. I don't mean that in the tabloid-conspiracy-theory, big-budget-horror-show, *Left Behind* sense of the word. Biblically, the Apocalypse is not about the

End of the World, but rather, as R.E.M. immortalized the phrase, "The End of the World As We Know It."

Christ's teaching about the Apocalypse is intimately tied to his teaching about the Kingdom of God. In simplest terms, we could say that the Kingdom of God is the world the way God wants it to be. It's the World As It Should Be. And it happens that the Kingdom of God is Jesus's number one discussion topic. (Since we're considering financial reparations, it's worth noting that his number two topic is: money and what we do with it.) The Apocalypse is the unfolding of the Kingdom into our own reality. Put another way, the Apocalypse is the World As It Is, becoming the World As It Should Be.

When we consider how riddled the Gospels are with stories of Jesus transgressing ethnicity, of his crossing cultural and national divisions to build relationship; when we consider how the Hebrew Scriptures highlight many similar transgressions throughout the whole history of God's relationship with the Israelites, it doesn't seem a stretch to propose that Racial Reconciliation, the transgression of our racial caste system, is part of God's plan for The World As It Should Be. Getting there is the hard part.

The lurid, sensationalist, and arresting imagery we associate with Apocalypticism (the kind of stuff you read in the Book of Revelation) is nothing more than the measure of that great distance between our reality, and God's hope for us. It is the measure of the kind of dramatic action that is necessary to get from where we are, to where we need to be. And this is what I mean when I say Racial Reconciliation requires an Apocalyptic reorganization of society. It will take some dramatic steps to get there.

Given how deeply we are divided by violent hierarchies of racial injustice, it does feel like it might require a cinematic-style Apocalypse to set things right: seas boiling, skies falling, sun turning to blood, Purple Rain, Stay-Puft Marshmallow Men, and all that.

Certainly, Jesus does talk about the Apocalypse this way sometimes. He describes the Kingdom coming like a thief in the night: unexpected and terrifying.

Ta-Nehisi Coates, himself an advocate for reparations, and a committed atheist, seems to envision something like this when he notes: "should white supremacy fall, the means by which that happens might be unthinkable to those of us bound by present realities and politics." We can't even see the way forward from the place where we now stand.

And yet, Coates does not take his epistemological pessimism on this point as an excuse for not doing the work. As he states: "Life is always a problem. The fact that … I don't necessarily see hope does not relieve people, does not relieve my son, does not relieve children of the responsibility to struggle." Coates expects, and exhorts, that we all must turn our feet, and trudge toward that longed for goal, even if it lies beyond the horizon of our imagination.

In this respect, as is often the case, one standing outside the faith of Christ models discipleship better than many of us who stand within. As a parishioner, Jennifer Amuzie, once told our gathered diocese: "No one needs Jesus more than Christians."

Jesus tells us Christians, again and again, that while the Kingdom of God may lie beyond our reach and imagination, it is not beyond the realm of our responsibility.

Our long slog of discipleship through the World As It Is feels immeasurably distant from the World As It Should Be. It may even feel like we're not making any progress. But Jesus reassures us that determined and persistent steps can yield startling results.

So, while he warns that the Kingdom will come like a thief in the night, he also encourages us, saying Kingdom is like yeast that slowly permeates a loaf of dough, until it is leavened throughout. He says the Kingdom is like a tiny seed that grows to become a mighty tree. Perhaps most significantly, he tells us that the Kingdom of God is in us. As Tolstoy observed, this teaching means, to some extent, that the Apocalyptic unfolding of the World As It Should Be is within our hands.

It's hard to reconcile a determined, life-long and persistent effort toward justice with the visions of catastrophic change St. John of Patmos describes in Revelation (the star Wormwood crashing down from the sky, turning all the rivers into gall, and whatnot). The first vision sounds progressive, the second revolutionary. How can they co-exist?

I'm not entirely sure, but I suspect it might look like this: if we ever got off our butts and committed, as a people, to the hard and enduring work of justice, for the long haul, then, over time, that work would become part of our identity. It would be who, and what we are. We would live in that strange space you experience when walking up a long hill. The beginning would be forgotten; the end would be out of sight. The climb would seem eternal and all-encompassing.

If we ever finally arrived at the summit of justice, we would be startled to realize that we had actually gotten there. We would feel that same dizzy, light-headed, wobbly-kneed confusion you experience when you realize your long slog is over.

No dollar amount can rightly account for, or make restitution for 400 years of brutal repression. We can't buy our way out of injustice. But money does matter. And money, real wealth, has the power to measurably improve a community's life. The Black community could do a lot with $14.25 trillion. That could represent home ownership, small business investments, education, health care, artists working without starving, and more.

It could represent something significant for the white community as well. A small out-of-pocket payment, a gift coming from discretionary funds, or a charitable offering made from surpluses can all be surrendered without undertaking substantial personal change. These kinds of transfers might become anecdotes in someone's story, but not part of their identity. I lament the time I rear-ended someone's car and was on the hook for the cost of their bumper. I'm a little ashamed of the time I spent too much on a set of juggling torches I didn't really need. But these moments don't define me. Writing off a few checks from budgetary surpluses could easily become a kind of wergild, an effort to buy our way to a clean conscience. That's certainly why I paid for that gentleman's rear bumper. I didn't want to have to think about it anymore.

But truly deep financial commitments (or liabilities), the kind that constitute a significant proportion of our assets, are different. Over time, they change how we think of ourselves. A woman paying out a 30-year mortgage is a homeowner. A man who donates 10% of his income every year is a tither. And a graduate staring down the barrel of $100k in student loans with no end in sight is a millennial. These are identity statements. They shape the decisions, relationships, and priorities we make.

A commitment of 14.7% of total assets could have a similar effect on white Americans. Getting to 14.7% would require serious soul-searching, a collective endeavor of wrestling with our history, hearing hard truths, embracing new possibilities and relationships. We would have to reconsider the patterns of our lives, and the ways we spend money. It will not be an easy road to get there. But, if we do, I suspect we will be surprised to find ourselves transformed by the journey. We might begin to think of ourselves as people confessing to, repenting of, and making restitution for white supremacy. We might decide to hold the institutions we belong to accountable, to change policies and practices, in alignment with our collective financial commitment. Again, as Jesus taught, "where your wealth is, there your heart will be also." He had a point.

For that teaching, we are bound to acknowledge that, while financial reparations alone cannot accomplish the work of Racial Reconciliation, any plan for reconciliation that does not include financial reparations is necessarily insincere.

And the process of paying reparations itself would create many opportunities for us (as a nation) to begin the work of reconciliation and community-building. Because to be considered genuine, restitution would necessarily have to fall under the direction and accountability of Black-led community organizations and institutions. Otherwise it wouldn't be restitution, it would be philanthropy: an effort to go on controlling our assets, even as we give them away. The administration and accountability of true restitution demands relationship.

Imagine that our businesses (large and small), governments (large and small), and community institutions and congregations (large and small) sat down with Black-led community organizations and institutions and said: "We'd like you to teach us what's owed. We'll pay it. You decide the best use for it. And, while you have no obligation to tell us, we are curious what you decide that best use is."

Now imagine if that last statement was offered, not with the interrogation of an auditor, but with the curiosity of a prospective friend, who genuinely wants to understand their neighbor's perspectives and priorities. What would be the result?

I really don't know. Certainly it would be messy, uncomfortable, and inconsistent. Tempers would flare. Some of us would say stupid things, and then we would have to apologize. We would have to do a lot of internal work to manage our own defensiveness. Some would balk, and complain after a few years (or just a few months) that enough had been done. We would have to keep reaffirming our collective commitment, again and again and again.

But suppose we stuck with it anyway. What would happen? The possibility fills me with wonder.

As this whole proposal depends heavily on that figure of 14.7%, let me make clear that I didn't pull the number out of a hat.

Many calculations for the value of reparations depend on estimating and totaling the value of the specific offenses (labor and land stolen, costs of predatory lending practices, etc.). I suspect this method of calculation derives from an interest in demonstrating, accounting for, and telling the truth about the history of Black oppression. This is a worthwhile, and necessary, goal on its own terms. My colleague, The Rev. Dr. Gayle Fisher-Stewart, has impressed upon me the need to identify, claim, and confess the harms we participate in, with specificity and clarity.

Failing to learn and name the specific harms we have taken part in erases the actual experience of the very people to whom we confess we owe reparations. Abstractifying these injuries, grouping them into nebulous clouds of "Anti-Black Racism" or "White Supremacy," obscures the reality and lives of the people who endure them. Their stories must be told, and heard.

But if our objective, at this early stage, is simply to open our thinking and imagination so we are prepared to hear those stories, then there are other ways for us to consider what is owed.

The economist Dr. William Darity proposes that the racial wealth gap itself indicates the strictly financial debt owed in reparations. That is, if we assume the racial wealth gap is due to white supremacist sabotage, then the total value of the Black/white racial wealth gap itself is equal to the value of reparations owed.

More formally, in an equitable world, we could guess that the wealth owned and controlled by a given population could be predicted by some complicated formula involving the following factors: time, the vagaries of chance, and the size of that population. Without attempting to derive that formula, we can, nonetheless, consider the factors themselves.

Time is a major factor in amassing wealth. Even under ideal circumstances, it takes years to save up for the down payment on a house. Investment funds compound and pile up interest through the decades. Passing generations might (or might not) have the opportunity to pass down inheritances, giving their descendants a leg up in achieving their dreams of prosperity.

With regard to the question of time, people of African descent have lived on what would become U.S. soil since 1528, from the very beginning of large-scale European colonization. And, from an early date, they were here in significant numbers. So the communities of Black and white Americans have had essentially equal time to amass collective wealth.

Of course, there is an element of randomness that governs all our lives. The pursuit of wealth is not exempt from this. Depending on the historical period, an unexpected injury or accident might literally cripple a person's earning potential. A fire, a drought, or an earthquake could wipe out years of accumulated assets. A lottery ticket with the right numbers might change a family's fortunes definitively.

Considered individually, these factors carry great weight. But, in the aggregate, the law of averages suggests that, with any large sample, the effects of random chance should level out over time. Given that we're dealing with communities numbering in the tens of millions, and time measured in centuries, we can assume that any ups and downs of fortune that are truly random would even out between white and Black communities.

The relationship between population size and collective wealth is intuitive and straightforward. All things being equal, we would expect to see a direct correlation. In an equitable world, if a given demographic represented one third of a nation's population, we would expect them to control one third of that nation's wealth.

Regarding population size, since the founding of the United States, Black people have represented between 19% and 9% of the U.S. population, averaging out at about 13.5%, which is close to the current figure of 14.2%. So, with the factors of time, and random chance being equal between the Black and white communities, and with the Black community relatively close to its current population proportion of 14.2% throughout its more than four hundred years of history in this land, we would expect Black America to control 14.2% of the nation's wealth.

As of 2014 (the most recent figures available) the federal reserve estimates total U.S. wealth at about $124 trillion. So if there were no white supremacist sabotage, we would expect Black Americans to own, or direct 14.2% of that, or about $17.6 trillion.

I say own or direct, because, of course, not all the nation's wealth is owned, directly, by individuals. We can split the wealth up into private, corporate, government and nonprofit buckets (the last being of particular interest for churches). Corporate wealth is held in proxy for the individuals who own those corporations. So individual and corporate wealth are really just two flavors of private wealth. But government and nonprofit wealth is held, nominally, by the public at large. Still, anyone with eyes can see clearly that this wealth is directed unevenly for the benefit and interest of particular populations.

Given that private wealth buys access, influence, and elections, we would expect that the direction of government wealth reflects the ownership of individual wealth. That is, if a given population owns 10% of the total private wealth, we would expect that 10% of government wealth would also be directed for the benefit and interest of that population.

Given that nonprofit wealth is generated by donations, and donations wield huge influence over nonprofit priorities (as anyone working in a nonprofit can tell you), we would expect the same trend of orientation for nonprofit wealth that we predict for government wealth.

So, again, we would expect Black Americans to own or direct 14.2% of the total wealth in the nation, or about $17.6 trillion.

So, then we have to figure out how much wealth Black Americans actually own or control. This is a little tricky. The Federal Reserve publishes figures for average and median household worth by race, generated by large-scale survey data, but not for aggregate worth by racial community. So we have to estimate backward. According to their 2019 figures, the average (mean) U.S. household owns $748,800 in total assets. If this figure seems surprising, we should note that the median U.S. household owns only $121,700, a disparity reflecting the vast economic inequality of our nation. Since average (mean) wealth should be equal to the aggregate wealth of a population divided by its size, it is more useful for generating estimates of total wealth.

The average (mean) Black household owns $142,500 in total assets. That is, the mean Black household wealth is only about 19% of the national average. (The median Black household wealth follows the same trend, coming in at 19.8% of the national median. This implies a couple of things. First, if we examine the Black community in isolation, we can observe the same class-based inequalities we see in the country at large. But, if we consider the Black community as a whole, in relation to the nation at large, we can observe race-based inequalities from the top to the bottom. That is, either the average Black uber-rich person owns only about 19% of what the average uber-rich person owns, or Black are represented among the ranks of the uber-rich at one fifth the levels we would expect, or, most likely, some combination of these two. A cursory review of any listing of U.S. billionaires bears this out.)

So if, on average, Black households own only 19% of the national average in wealth, and if Black people represent 14.2% of the total population, and if the orientation of public wealth mirrors the ownership of private wealth, then we can assume that the Black community owns, or directs 19% times 14.2% times $124 trillion. Which is about $3.35 trillion. This is about $14.25 trillion less than what we would have expected, all things being equal.

So, what's not equal? What accounts for the Black community being $14.25 trillion behind? A discrepancy that large demands explanation. As we consider that gap we are faced with a choice, and it is a vitally important one:

Either we acknowledge that the Black community has been systemically plundered, and that that plunder deserves restitution, or we persist in the belief that there is something deficient about Black people. Squarely facing the reality of the wealth gap demands that we choose between an anti-racist and a white supremacist explanation. And it makes clear that there is no middle ground between them.

Many, perhaps most, Americans like to believe that we live in a meritocracy. We like to believe that financial success is largely a matter of personal drive, ability, and fitness. The idea is comforting because it allows us to believe we have definitive control over our financial situation. It teaches us that everything we possess is ours by right, that we have earned it. I think there's good factual reason to doubt the truth behind this belief. There's good scriptural reason too: Jesus, Amos, Isaiah and the authors of Ecclesiastes and Job all reject the idea that wealth is tied to personal virtue.

But just as importantly, there is good moral reason to reject this idea. Because, if we apply the idea of a meritocracy to the racial wealth gap, we are left with the impression that there is something internally wrong with the Black community. That is, if we allow ourselves to believe that wealth is a product of drive, ability, and fitness, and if we acknowledge the simple fact that the Black community collectively is financially impoverished, then we will conclude that the Black community is somehow lacking in drive, ability, and fitness. In essence, when faced with the reality of the racial wealth gap, our commitment to the idea of a meritocracy obliges us to hold racist ideas about the inferiority of Black people.

And this is more than just theory. I suspect when most of us (white, Black, or otherwise) witness the impoverishment of many Black communities, some part or corner of our mind tells us that it is somehow their fault. Perhaps, like enslavers before us, we tell ourselves they are deficient, morally, intellectually, or otherwise. Perhaps we hold to Daniel Patrick Moynihan's mythology of families pathologically led by single Black mothers. Perhaps we carry these beliefs with bile and hatred. Maybe we hold them with patronizing pity. Maybe we proclaim these beliefs publicly, feeling justified. Maybe we keep them to ourselves, thinking it's not polite to say such things out loud. Regardless, our trust is in meritocracy, our assumption is that wealth is the result of "good choices," and our suspicion is that somehow poor Black communities are responsible for the poverty that afflicts them. These are all racist beliefs.

In fact, on average, the abilities and drives of any two given human populations are equal. This is true not only as a matter of solid scientific evidence (which supports the claim). It is true not only as a matter of experiential/anecdotal witness (which reveals the truth in every moment we are able to look beyond our biases and see the people around us as they are, and not as we imagine them to be). It is true also as a matter of anti-racist conviction, that no reasonable moral system can allow us to reject.

How then, will we account for the vast disparity between the expected and actual wealth of the Black community? If it is not the result of an internal factor, then it must arise from an external source. Even a cursory survey of history will reveal the truth: the impoverishment of Black communities is the result of white supremacist sabotage and theft:

Whereas white Americans stole property and land upon their arrival on these shores, Black Americans were stripped of their property and land before getting here.

Whereas white Americans have been, and still are, privileged when it comes to hiring, promotion, home ownership, access to credit and more, Black Americans were, and are, systematically denied such opportunities.

Whereas white Americans were, generally, protected by the nation's legal, police and military structure, Black Americans have been subject to chattel slavery, lynching, and the carcel state, all of which, beyond their human horror, have profoundly adverse economic consequences.

The wealth gap represents the financial legacy of white supremacy. That difference of $14.25 trillion between the $17.6 trillion expected total Black wealth and the $3.35 trillion dollars actual total Black wealth is the amount that must be repaired. It is the value of reparations owed.

It's always good to check your work against other estimates. In this case, a review of scholarship regarding the value of reparations owed yields figures between $5 and $17 trillion. This proposed estimate of $14.25 trillion falls comfortably in the middle of that range, which is encouraging. We can plausibly call it the value of white sabotage and theft.

I say sabotage and theft, because it is important to recognize that racism is not simply an affliction against communities of color, but also a mechanism for enriching white communities. It is with good reason that Ta-Nehisi Coates prefers the term "plunder" when describing the action of white supremacist structures. Riches piled up from enslavement became the starting capital for hedge funds and endowments that grew into the wealth inherited by white individuals and institutions today. Discriminatory hiring practices offered whites opportunities to increase their income, precisely as, and often because, Blacks were denied these positions. Predatory lending practices, eminent domain, and "urban renewal" stripped Black families of real estate, turning it over to white hands, even as the value of that property skyrocketed.

To say that Black communities have suffered unjust hardship is to tell only half the story. It is more honest to say that white communities have unjustly enriched themselves through the unjust deprivation of Black communities. This is theft.

That theft is borne out by the numbers. The average (mean) white household owns $983,400 in total assets. This is about 31% above the national average. Similarly, the median white household's net worth is $188,200, about 55% above the national median. Just as the Black community's grossly diminished wealth demands explanation, so too does the white community's dramatically inflated net worth. How can we explain this?

Any explanation that resorts, or alludes, to ideas of special virtue, or drive, or ability on the part of the white community must be acknowledged as racist, per se. That is, such explanations require explicitly adopting belief in white superiority.

If we eliminate this explanation, and we acknowledge that random chance should level out for a population this large, we are left with the inevitable conclusion that the white community has enriched itself at the expense of the Black community (and of other communities of color as well). White Americans are the only racial group with average wealth above the national average. All other racial groups have wealth below the national average. Theft.

And this is where, for white Americans, the question of the wealth gap becomes personal. It is one thing for us to look at the impoverishment of the Black community and admit that we are seeing the results of sabotage. It's another to look at the equity of our own homes, our savings accounts, and pension funds, and recognize the old, subtle, and complex network of channels that pulls wealth from Black communities and deposits it into our hands.

This is what financial reparations are all about. They are not a matter of paying for the guilt of past injuries and harms. Those debts can never be paid in cash. Enslavement, rape, dehumanization, othering: these require different kinds of commitments, different processes of healing, restoration and reparation.

Financial reparations are, to some extent, a matter of mere accounting. They are seeing and acknowledging that we, white Americans, hold financial assets that are not our own, assets that have been taken, or stolen, from the people who earned and built them. Those assets must be returned.

What would that look like in real terms? Let's apply the same logic we used to estimate the total wealth held or directed by Black Americans. We can begin by considering that the average (mean) white household owns $983,400, with a median wealth of $188,200. These figures are 131% and 155% of the national figures, respectively. White people represent about 62% of the U.S. population. And with the average white household holding 131% of the national average (mean) in terms of wealth, we could guess that white people control about 61% of 131% of the nation's wealth, or about 80%, which is about $99 trillion dollars. The $14.6 trillion owed in reparations constitutes about 14.7% of that total. That is, about 14.7% of white net worth in this country is owed in reparations. Because their assets have been drawn from private white wealth, predominantly white institutions (including churches) should consider themselves on the hook for the same total.

The idea of reparations raises many logistical hurdles. Who gets reparations? Are all white people equally complicit, and thus equally responsible for payment? How is it paid out and administered? These are complicated, tangled problems. But we (and here I mean, we, the nation) have untangled complicated problems before.

In every case, we did it by first deciding that the problem needed to be solved, and then figuring out how to solve it. When President John F. Kennedy announced that we would put a man on the moon, NASA hadn't even completed a full manned orbit of the earth. We set the goal of the moon before we could imagine the solution for getting there. If we try to find solutions before committing to the goal, we will perceive every problem as an insurmountable roadblock, not as a hurdle to overcome. We will find ten thousand reasons to never get started.

As a society, we haven't even gotten as far as deciding that the logistics of reparations are worth untangling. We haven't yet committed to the goal. And despite this reticence, there are a great number of Black scholars who have already proposed a variety of possible solutions to all of these thorny questions. None of the logistical hurdles are insurmountable. We just have to commit to overcoming them. The first job, then, is to build political will for the payment of reparations.

Churches are well suited to this task, and can do it leading by example. Assessing reparations based on the wealth of white individuals, predominantly white businesses, and predominantly white government entities is properly the work of local, state and federal governments themselves. The existing channels of taxation and appropriation are well suited to the purpose. Governments have the resources to document, measure and consider models for paying reparations robustly and thoroughly. And the collective mechanism of taxation and appropriation would offer a bulwark against reparations becoming a hodge-podge of individualistic philanthropic pet projects.

But public nonprofits, like churches, handle their wealth and finances on a largely volitional basis. They aren't subject to taxation or appropriation. And while, arguably, this can lead to a lack of accountability, there is also a wonderful freedom in it. We could begin the work right now. And in doing so, we could begin a moral movement that might push national political discourse around reparations. We could get the ball rolling. It might not even be that hard.

Does your predominantly white church or community organization want to take the first step on reparations?

Assess your wealth. A quick look at bank and endowment statements, real property assessments at your local registry of deeds, and your insurance policy coverage could give you a reasonable estimate with only a couple hours of work.

Find a Black-led community organization or church in your area with a track record of commitment to their community. Ideally, find one whose perspective on community uplift challenges you. Call them up, arrange a meeting, explain you're planning to commit 14.7% of your church's assets toward reparations. This conversation may be uncomfortable. That's okay. It will make you stronger.

Explain to your folk how this is a necessary step toward the vision of Racial Reconciliation. Learn, and teach the abundant evidence describing how systemic inequality sabotages economic well-being, political stability, and intellectual innovation for everyone in societies where it exists. Help your folk see how committing to address white supremacist sabotage, and committing to sacrifice for the safety, health and freedom of Black communities (as defined on their own terms) promotes a safer, healthier, freer, and wiser society for us all.

And then tell other churches what you're doing. Maybe people will start to ask questions. You'll be planting a mustard seed. Maybe another white church will be inspired by your example. And if enough white churches in your area begin to act, maybe they'll start to ask why white-owned companies in the area aren't doing the same. Maybe that seed will start to grow.

I admit, alongside wonder, that the prospect of this work incites some trepidation in me. It draws attention to other uncomfortable questions. In particular, when we consider the question of reparations to Black Americans, it is hard not to ask ourselves, "What about reparations to Native Americans?" And in considering that question, all the math I can envision ends with the same solution: making just reparation to Native Americans would require handing over everything, the whole nation and all its wealth. And personally, I can't picture a means toward that outcome which does not involve the Four Horsemen of the Apocalypse.

Perhaps the problem is not the question itself, but rather the limits of my imagination. We must not allow our failures of imagination to limit our calling.

When I first considered that figure of 14.7% it seemed so intimidating, that I tried to soften it to make it more manageable and palatable. I suggested amortizing it over thirty years, after the fashion of a mortgage. The resulting schedule of annual payments, amounting to just 1.5% of each white family or institution's income seemed achievable, easily so even. I thought it was a clever idea.

Jennifer Amuzie, the same parishioner who noted that no one needs Jesus more than Christians, pushed back on my (admittedly self-satisfied) cleverness:

"When you posted this I felt a little ambivalent about the numbers. And witnessing a year where one in 1000 Black Americans died preventable deaths from COVID has really galvanized me: this is too small and too slow. We don't have 30 years to get this right. No other group that was offered reparations had a generations-long installment plan. I'm also reminded that the Episcopal Church committed 0.7% of its budget to the Millennial Development Goals 15 years ago and fell short of that. America's racial reckoning, the church's reckoning, shouldn't look like setting and missing unambitious goals."

Confronted by her criticism, which was on point, I realized I had been trying to conform the facts of these difficult numbers to my own comfort, and the limits of my own imagination, which isn't something Christians should do. If faith means anything, it must mean embracing truths beyond the bounds of our imagination, or else it is not faith at all.

That faith will be important as we continue on. Reparations aim to restore something that has never been whole: justice and relationship across race in this nation. We are therefore, in some sense, venturing into the unknown.

In more specific terms, for those of us who are white, the work of reparations requires us to hear, and receive, wisdom from Black people who've been at this work for years. You'll be hearing some of that wisdom in the pages that follow. This wisdom will often challenge our own assumptions and conceptions. Amuzie's criticism was just such a challenge for me. We must be prepared to embrace these challenges. I hope this exercise has stretched you a little bit for the work to come.

2

A Process
in Six Stages

Pulling from the counsel and insights of nine teachers you'll be meeting shortly, I propose a basic framework for a six-stage process toward reparations. The sequencing of these stages is important, but in reality, even with the best preparation and planning, we are all feeling our way forward in the reparations process. Inevitably, we'll find ourselves looping back, to revisit stages we'd thought we'd covered, or skipping ahead before we're ready. Give yourself grace when making missteps. Don't dwell on them too heavily. But learn from them, and be more thorough as you continue.

Our process within the Reparations Task Force of the EDOW has been one of failing our way forward. At each stage, we had grand ideas for reparations, which we rushed to complete, only to notice essential groundwork we'd neglected in our haste. My hope is that you'll benefit from the learnings of our hindsight and the mistakes we've made along the way.

The six stages of the process I suggest mirror the implied steps of the rite of repentance and reconciliation, what many call the sacrament of confession. As an Episcopalian, I reflexively relate everything to the prayer book and our liturgy, but in this case I think it works.

These six stages are as follows:

1. Relationship
2. Truth-Finding
3. Truth-Telling
4. Repentance
5. Reparation
6. Evaluation

Those of you who are familiar with the sacrament of confession were probably looking for stages like "Reconciliation" or "Forgiveness." I'll address those questions at the end of the book. In my understanding, they are connected to this process, though they aren't properly part of it. I'll explain why later. For now, let's consider each of these six stages in turn. At the end of each section, I'll suggest a few next steps, to get you, and your congregation, or institution started in the process.

We're coming now to the heart of this book: the words, counsel and advice of people who are doing the work. Before you meet them, I want to offer a brief disclaimer.

Fisher-Stewart, my most consistent dialogue partner in this work, once told me at a predominantly white gathering, "you made this mess, you have to clean it up." There is truth in that. The hurts of white supremacy and anti-Black racism are ones that our people created. It is our responsibility to uncreate them. We must do the work. At the same time, in confronting and dismantling white supremacy, in making repair for four hundred years of injury, we must follow guidance and counsel from people of color who know first-hand what the mess looks like.

This tension, between taking initiative in confronting the problems we participate in and perpetuate, and following the lead of those directly impacted, is only one of many contradictions we will encounter as we continue the work. You may notice that the teachers we're about to meet don't concur on all points (though I am surprised by how many core themes they agree about). In some places they differ markedly from one another.

As Fisher-Stewart rightly framed it, the legacy of white supremacy is a colossal mess. At our home, on cleaning days, I put on a special set of clothes. They're stained, bleach-marked and worn. I put these clothes on because inevitably, when you clean, you get dirty. There's no way around it.

If we're serious about this business of cleaning up the mess of racist harms, if we're serious about reparations, we need to be ready to get messy. There are no clean-cut answers. They will all be messy and imperfect. But we cannot take this as an excuse for moral solipsism. There are real truths. There are best practices we can, and must, learn. But we're going to have to wade into the messiness of it, and get our hands dirty, if we hope to learn them.

CHAPTER

3

Building Relationship

Foundational to the sacrament of confession is the idea that both harm, and healing happen in a relationship. When we confess our sins saying: "We have not loved [God] with our whole heart. We have not loved our neighbors as ourselves" (BCP, 360), the sins we confess are breaches and fractures of relationship, whether it be our relationship with God, or our relationship with the people around us. And scripture makes plain that our relationship with God, and our relationship with neighbors are inextricably linked. Jesus teaches us that loving our neighbor is "like" loving God (Matt. 22:39). John challenges that it is impossible to love God, who we can't see, if we don't love the people around us, who we do see (1 John 4:20). That is to say, the breaches and fractures in our relationship with our neighbors are, by definition, sins against God.

White supremacy is no exception to this rule. Discussions around racism in recent decades have shifted our focus away from personal biases, and toward systemic and systematic harms. This is an appropriate, and important, shift. By the numbers, the greatest injuries of white supremacy aren't perpetrated by bed-sheet wearing bigots, but by polite bureaucrats and sweet mannered committee chairs, pleasantly turning the well-oiled gears of our society's racial meat-grinder.

29

And yet, there is a danger that our discourse around systemic racism will disengage us from, and abstractify, our relationship with those systems. Structural racism persists, because we (principally white people) participate in, support, and recreate these structures on a daily basis. We do it in our church personnel committees when we favor "people like us" with hiring recommendations. We do it in our choirs and altar guilds when we uncritically, and exclusively, lift up expressions of white European culture because "that's just who we are." We do this when we develop policies for handling "disruptive visitors" that include calling the police. We create these structures, and in every case there are people, specific individuals with stories all their own, on the receiving end of injuries we are unconsciously inflicting.

The harms of white supremacy always occur in relationships. Repair for those harms must occur in relationships as well. There is a reason we make our confession communally each Sunday. Even individual confession is always offered with someone else in the room. And any pastor worth their salt will advise folks confessing that true penance requires reaching out to those we have harmed, apologizing and making restitution in so far as is possible, without causing further harm.

This is more than mere theological navel-gazing. It is a deeply practical matter. Our EDOW Reparations Task Force started in this work trying to reinvent the wheel. We had been at our task for more than a year when it occurred to us that there were quite a few institutions around the country who had undertaken their own reparations initiatives, some of whom had several years of experience in this work, and that we could learn from their efforts.

We commissioned a researcher, Cane West, to survey these initiatives, nation-wide. He identified seventy projects from

institutions around the country, universities, churches, municipalities, and others, that had labeled themselves "reparations."
The resulting raw data set is daunting. We parsed it out by
the response of the community directly impacted, that is, the
people to whom each institution determined they owed reparations. We identified two groups within the data, which we
coarsely marked as "failures" and "successes."

We defined failures as those projects that were roundly
rejected by the directly impacted community. This group of
projects frequently received comments of the sort "they need
to scrap it all and start over," or "it would've been better if they
hadn't done anything."

We defined success as those projects that received substantial constructive criticism from the directly impacted community. These projects were met with a sense of qualified welcome:
appreciation for what was being done, alongside criticism for
what could be done better. We took this as a potential indicator
of genuine engagement and investment in the project on the
part of the directly impacted community.

We asked West to identify, if possible, commonalities
among the two groups. We were curious to know which practices lead to a project the community embraces, versus one
they reject. He's still analyzing the data, but one factor jumps
out immediately after a cursory review: successful projects had
early and deep engagement with directly-impacted communities. Failed projects had little or none. Again, the harms of
white supremacy occur in relationship, its remedies must come
in relationship as well.

The first relationships you'll need to form for this work are
internal. Your congregational reparations work will be doomed
to fail if it becomes the pet project of one member. You will
need a community to join you in this work.

Susan Schulken was one of the original members of the book reading group that grew into the EDOW's Reparations Task Force and she has continued to work with the task force. She is a member of Wade in the Water, the racial justice ministry of Grace Episcopal Church in Silver Spring, Maryland, and leads their Parish History of Race and Racism team. She has one of the strongest and most principled commitments to internal anti-racist work of any white person I've met. She describes the importance of community support in this work.

> *It's good to have people to work with. I was drawn to Grace Church because they had an active racial justice ministry. Not a social justice ministry, but specifically a racial justice ministry, with Black folks and white folks who are coming at this issue from all different perspectives and different experiences, but all of whom have a commitment to educating our parish. That was a priority. Because though we're a fairly diverse parish, we did have work to do. And we still do. The racial justice group recognizes that. It's been very supportive, and I've learned a lot through being a part of the group.*

Schulken's focus for the last year, as an outgrowth of the Task Force's work, has been her parish's history with racism. She helped form and leads a new working group that was initially all white. But she looked for someone to be the conscience of that group, to help keep them honest. And she knew that that person needed to be Black. A member of the congregation volunteered to stand in the role, and Schulken has worked to continue building that relationship.

The most important relationships to build are those with the community outside your congregation. These are the relationships that will hold you accountable. It's one thing to acknowledge the fault in our own minds. It's quite another to speak with the people we've wronged, and hear from them what harms were done. Doing so often requires relinquishing our own assumptions and understandings. I imagine we've all had the experience of saying sorry, only to have someone tell us what we apologized for was not the real problem; our true offense was something else entirely. As is true for many Episcopal priests, I don't receive private confession all that often. But I do it enough to notice patterns. One thing I've learned is this: we look at our offenses through the lens of our own sensitivities.

This is partly the training of our faith. After all, Jesus teaches us "in everything do to others what you would have them do to you" (Matt. 7:12). We make assumptions about what would hurt others, or not, based on what would hurt us. But where differences in culture, experience and socio-economic circumstances are wide, as is often the case when we come to discuss reparations, these assumptions will frequently prove false. We need the teaching of the very people we have harmed to truly understand what harms we have committed. Seeking repair in relationship is difficult, and requires a degree of surrender.

Building relationships, especially the kind within which repair can take place, is not a paint-by-numbers endeavor. There are no step-by-step instructions on how to proceed. But there are some good places to start. There's value in being willing to just put yourself out there. If you're thinking of taking on reparations work in your local congregation, once you've made a guess about the community to whom you owe reparations, probably the most important thing you could do is to reach out to representatives of that community, begin a conversation and start building relationship. This takes time, and a commitment to simply show up. The work may not be as flashy or dramatic as making bold public statements, or drafting institution-shaking policy, but it is where genuine change begins.

Natacia Knapper is an organizer with Washington, DC's mutual aid networks, and the Managing Organizer for the American Civil Liberties Union (ACLU) in DC. The personal witness of their life and work demonstrates how relationship is the foundation for all genuinely transformative action.

> *I've been in Washington, DC, about 15 years or so. I live in the Ward One community, and as a resident here I do mutual aid organizing in a personal capacity as part of the DC Mutual Aid Network, but more specifically with Ward One Mutual Aid. My work with that group looks like a lot of different things. It means having kind of regular meetings with my pod, that is, my neighbors that live in close proximity to me in Ward One and creating a network of care. That means checking in on each other, figuring out what needs aren't being met, and helping folks get connected to resources, if I can. Sometimes it's not so much about creating resources. It's about just being able to be there to listen to the hardships people are going through, and just lending an ear and support for folks.*

Knapper's work has also focused on tenant organizing and housing justice. With a group of Ward One Mutual Aid organizers, she is currently attempting to purchase their apartment building and convert it into a housing co-op that will create permanent, safe, clean, long-term housing in the neighborhood. Knapper deeply impresses me with their holistic and multi-layered approach to the work of justice. They advocate at the national and municipal level and organize in their own neighborhood. They take on grand endeavors, like purchasing and collectivizing their apartment building, and give equal care to small, routine acts of community care:

Once a month me and a few of my neighbors get together and do a table in the U Street area, where we provide hot meals, donated goods, toiletries and whatever other items of support that would be useful to our unhoused neighbors.

All these efforts are threads in a single tapestry of care. All are focused on building relationships with a community that often gets forgotten.

I want us to notice how, as Knapper describes it, the work of building relationships, and the work of creating transformative change interweave seamlessly. If we're serious about reparations, if we're serious about repair, we must learn to emulate this attitude. The first step in making reparation is building relationship with those we've harmed.

There's a danger here of trying to draft people we know well, with whom we're comfortable, into work they might not willingly choose. Bearing witness to the harms of racism is unpleasant work many people of color would rather not take on. Being the targets of racist harm, this is entirely their right. They have no obligation to participate. Whereas those of us who are white, who benefit from systems of systems of racist oppression, have a moral imperative not to look away from the harm these systems inflict. So we find ourselves between a rock and a hard place. We need the guidance and direction of people of color to accurately identify the racist harms we inflicted, and what remedies might be appropriate. But we must also respect the choice some people of color will make, for their own good reasons, to refuse offering guidance and direction.

For white churches, one solution to this quandary is to seek out those who've made it their business to face and tackle these ugly truths. Wherever you find yourself in this country there are Black- and brown-led organizations working to confront and remedy racialized inequities in your community. A simple internet search will give you a place to start. Ideally, you'll want to approach an organization whose politics and power analysis make you at least a little uncomfortable. They will help stretch you toward the truth.

Send an email, make a call. Tell them your church is interested in tackling the question of reparations, and you're looking for a partner with expertise and skin in the game to point out your blind spots and keep you accountable. From personal experience I can tell you, this conversation will be deeply uncomfortable. Learn to get comfortable with your discomfort. They may flatly turn you down. This is okay. It is their right. Thank them for their time and keep looking. Make another call, send another email.

Sooner or later you'll meet a community leader who is interested in what you're doing. They may ask you tough questions about your church, your project, the specifics of the relationship you're proposing, or your own seriousness and commitment. Answer with all the honesty you can muster, be as flexible as you are able. Don't be afraid to say "I don't know" or "I haven't thought about that." A deep commitment to listen will be your most important discipline at this stage. Everyone I've spoken to about this work emphasized the importance of listening.

The Rev. Deacon Antonio Baxter, is deeply committed to the growth of Black churches, having launched and worked on a variety of initiatives to promote their vitality. He approaches the work of reparations from that vantage point. He poignantly frames the need to listen in this work:

> Spend a lot of time listening, to hear the stories. Some of them are going to be ugly.

So in order to have this conversation, you have to be willing to listen, and be slow to react. You can't listen from the posture of defensiveness. You have to listen to truly hear the story, and the impact of racism and what it's done to people psychologically and economically, then place yourself in those stories, so as to feel what you might feel if you were there.

When you do that, you'll know why you're doing the work. And even when you feel discouraged, that will keep you wanting to repair the damage that's been done.

As Baxter suggests, while you're building these relationships of accountability for the work of reparations, you'll need to commit to manage your own defensiveness, and just listen. This is not only a humbling experience but also one that requires us to proactively develop the discipline of humility.

Lindsay Ayers is policy counsel for DC Justice Lab, an advocacy group working on large-scale reforms in Washington, DC's legal and criminal systems. Ayers put her finger precisely on the kind of humility required in this work, especially for white people:

First and foremost, you need to approach the work with humility. In my experience working with white people, a lot of times there's a feeling of assumed authority. Because when people are always in charge, they're always centered in the conversation, historically and practically. We always default to whiteness. When white people are coming into these spaces they need to be mindful of the weight their whiteness carries. And be intentional about decentering themselves.

Ayers says that there's a respectful way to come into the conversation. Listening always goes well for her.

I recommend to white people that you listen first and speak sec-ond. I would like to see people coming into this space with an honest desire to learn, not to assuage white guilt. I understand that it's a real thing. But it's not mine to carry, it's not ours to carry as Black people. That's between you and the Lord or them, or you and yourselves.

She recommends entering with curiosity, humility, and openness, listening deeply, then sharing and contributing after trust has been built.

Developing that discipline of humility and listening will serve you well throughout the entire process. These conversations will be a good time to begin practicing it. As the conversation ends, ask this question: "Who else should I talk with about this?"

Bit by bit, you'll work together to form a group that can guide you and keep you accountable in your efforts. Inter-personal relationships will be foundational as the group forms. There is no substitute for those one-to-one, face-to-face conversations. But, at the same time, you'll also be building inter-communal relationships: that is, relationships between your two distinct communities, the community that has inflicted harm, and the community that has been harmed, as whole communities. Some white people (myself included), may find themselves unaccustomed to thinking about relationships in these communal terms. Like many white people, I've been socialized to think at the individual level. I'll generally try to mentally separate the person I'm speaking with from whatever community they may belong to. There can be a good reason to do this. It might save us from that biased tendency to imagine someone else as just another representative "their group." But the problem is, in their uniqueness and distinctiveness, many people choose communal identity as a fundamental touch-stone of who they are. Which means that when we stubbornly insist on meeting people strictly as individuals, we ironically end up denying the individuality of people with a strong sense of communal identity.

Moreover, whether we acknowledge it or not, we often have a self-serving agenda when we prioritize interpersonal relationships over and against intercommunal relationships. Given the diversity of thought in our human family, it is always possible to find people, within any group, who will willingly let us off the hook. There are queer folks who will excuse my homophobic bias, and trans-folk who will dismiss my unconscious transphobia, and women who deny the patriarchal patterns of my life, and Black people who will tell me my participation is white supremacy is not a real thing. We can selectively choose relationships that will support us in the choices we've already made. Intercommunal relationships bring a different aspect of accountability.

The Rev. Grey Maggiano told me a bit about what this looks like. Maggiano is the rector of Memorial Episcopal Church in Baltimore. While the Episcopal Diocese of Maryland took on a commitment to reparations at the diocesan level, Maggiano led his congregation to make a remarkable commitment of its own: 10% of its endowment to be paid in reparations over five years. They've been delivering on it. Outside Memorial, there's a banner hanging that reads "Black Neighborhoods Matter." I asked Maggiano about it:

> *The tagline is not ours. It was developed locally by author and activist Lawrence Brown, who has written a book called The Black Butterfly and has done a lot of research on segregation*

in Baltimore, along with some other folks. He's been leading an
effort to set up a Black neighborhoods reparations fund.

Maggiano explained that because the racism in Baltimore is structural and so ingrained to the system, that it's not enough to say, "Well, we just need to make it easier for individual Black people to succeed." Targeted investment is needed in the communities that have been strategically disinvested in.

Memorial has also identified four areas where they recognized their church has done substantial harm in the past:

So we're going to focus on those four areas, and we're going to
do that within the same ZIP code as the church. Because that is
roughly where our church had the greatest negative impact.

Coming back to the banner, he explained:

The sign used to say Black lives matter. And it was getting tat-
tered and worn down.

He approached the church's reparations committee, composed
of both church and community members, to get recommendations
on what to do with the aging banner. After hearing recommen-
dations for a variety of art installations to replace the banner,
three members of the wider community spoke:

"Just say, 'Black Neighborhoods Matter.' That's the sign we
all have in our front yards. If you spend more time on this, you're
taking time away from actually making Black neighborhoods
matter."

That criticism, the push to get back to the work, is a kind of accountability that often shows up in intercommunal relationships. Memorial had access to this vital and urgent accountability, precisely because they'd made a choice to enter into relationship with the neighborhood immediately around them: not only one-to-one as individuals, but also community-to-community.

You'll need to negotiate the boundaries, shared expectations and norms of your relationship together. Habits of regular reporting, transparency and responsiveness will be essential. You may find some Black-led organizations working on questions of racial justice will approach the idea of partnering with predominantly white institutions skeptically. This may be true even of those organizations that are willing to consider the possibility. It's important to respect this skepticism as a rational response to a long history of predominantly white institutions setting unambitious goals and breaking promises in their effort at racial justice.

Ayers, who is Black, shared the skepticism she experienced, as she approached members of DC's Black community with similar questions.

> *I haven't experienced anything adverse. But I feel like there is always a thin layer of skepticism. People will ask, "Where are you from? You don't sound like you're from around here." I welcome those questions. That's how you build relationship. People are open to sharing. They're curious about who I am and why I'm asking, but they do want people to know what DC Black residents are experiencing. They want their voices to be heard. And they see us coming here for jobs, without knowing where we're landing. Without knowing the history. So there's skepticism.*

I would suggest the most productive way to encounter this skepticism is to acknowledge and speak to it directly.

At the Task Force's first joint meeting with our Accountability Board, we asked each accountability board partner to answer two questions:

Imagine it's two years from now, and we've been meeting together for an hour, once a month, during that time:
  1. *What outcomes would you need to see to be able to say this was a good use of your time, and you are glad you decided to participate?*
  2. *What outcomes would lead you to say this was not a good use of your time, and you regret participating?*

By naming both possibilities, and inviting response, we were able to acknowledge and respect the reasonable skepticism of our partners, and receive constructive feedback on guidelines for achieving a better result. Baxter's response to that question highlight's both the potentials and pitfalls of this work:

This will be a good use of my time if it leads to a robust discussion about the damage done and how to repair it, if the church honestly accounts for its part in slavery, or racism inflicted on the larger community. But, if we only focus on the larger community, if we don't look at how it impacted our own institutions, our Black churches, I will be disappointed. It will be a bad use of my time if this comes off as a PR stunt. It would be a bad use of my time if we don't consider the spiritual impact of past wrongs. We must consider the spiritual impact as well, because we're followers of Jesus Christ. Because we believe that when you wrong your brother, you have to try and make it right, you have to go and ask forgiveness. Lastly, if decisions about reparations are made from the top down and not from the bottom up, organically, that would be a waste of my time.

Your accountability partners may decide they want to meet without you, or your church members, present. This might make you uneasy. You may find yourself wondering what they're talking about when you aren't around. As much as you are able, put these cares and questions aside. Monocultural spaces are both necessary and desirable. Baxter describes the importance of these spaces, for self-identified Black congregations:

> *To be clear, these churches, Black churches, are open to all people, and invite anyone who wants to come and be a part of the work that they're doing. We want to be welcoming. We want reconciliation. But there is a unique characteristic to the institution of the Black church, which you certainly don't want to lose.*
>
> *The Black church has given hope and a positive identity and image to people who didn't always get that. We may think that this may not be so important now, but when you look at what's going on in our communities you can see that picture of a positive identity still needs to be painted today.*

Monocultural spaces provide those engaged in deeply vulnerable conversations the opportunity to share freely without being scrutinized. They create opportunities to express oneself in the short-hand of common experience, without being required to offer exposition. Whatever discomfort you may feel, ultimately, you must make a choice to trust the partners you've invited to keep you accountable.

In the EDOW, we've sought out accountability partners who represent a variety Black-led organizations working on liberation, economic empowerment, and structures of care in the Black community. Our partners gather each month, at an accountability board they convene themselves. Liaisons from the Reparations Task Force join this meeting for this first half hour, to present updates, take feedback and questions, and bring requests and challenges back to the Task Force. Then we recuse ourselves, allowing the accountability to caucus for the second half hour. Our relationship has not been without conflict or tension. This is to be expected. Building relationship isn't always easy. But it is necessary for the work of reparations to have integrity.

I list building relationship as the first stage, because it must be where our work begins. It is also the place where genuine transformation occurs.

Dr. Jocelyn Imani is a community historian who has worked with the National Museum of African American History and Culture, the National Park Service, and the Trust for Public Land. She's the founder and organizer of the Big Brown Get Down, a networking event designed to connect middle and high school scholars with mentors for the purpose of providing them with exposure and opportunity. She describes, from personal experience, what relational transformation can look like:

> I'm not going to lie. A lot of the time these people don't get me. They don't go past the surface to see the layers of that underneath. That's frustrating. But they live in that experience too. They're also only seen on the surface level. We live in such a wicked broken world, that for most people it's a very foreign experience to be treated with grace and kindness.

For Imani, approaching others in a spirit of compassion has opened opportunities for new learning. She came to recognize that the same systemic conditions that keep Black people down, also keep poor white people in poverty: the same monster of white supremacy.

> When you're deep in your sickness—and I really do see white supremacy as, at best, an illness, and at worst a demonic spirit—you're in it so deep, you're blinded by it.

In Imani's experience, compassion is the antidote for the sickness and shame of white supremacy. She acknowledges that this strategy hasn't always turned out well. She has had people return her kindness with evil. But she accepts whatever response comes with faith.

> *That's between you and God. It doesn't have anything to do with me. But sometimes, when I tell people the truth in that uncompromising way, and tell it with kindness, I see their hearts soften. Kindness is a seed that's planted. Something good will come of it.*

You'll need to establish relationship as a touchstone value in your reparations work, and continue returning to it. As you move into the phase of shaping reparations policies for your organization, it can be very tempting to let calls for efficiency override the demands of connection. Ayers lays out the dangers of that temptation:

> *The people aspect for me has to come first. Policy must come second to the emotional side of reparations. Most of the work that we do at DC Justice Lab has an emotional component that can't be taken out of the policy. With reparations, that runs really deep. These are generational wounds that we're trying to address.*

For Ayers,

> *No good policy comes from unimpacted people dreaming it up themselves. Centering the experiences, the emotions, the grief, the trauma, and the ideas of those who've been harmed, the people who would be the beneficiaries of repair, is the only way to create policy that actually impacts and solves the problem addressed.*

Relationships with those our institutions have directly harmed must undergird everything that follows, or the work can have no integrity at all.

CHAPTER

4

Truth-Finding

Gayle Fisher-Stewart taught me, "Before you get to truth-telling, you've got to go through the work of truth-finding." As you're forming and building relationships of accountability, your next task will be to investigate and uncover what harms have been done. This stage may seem obvious: How can you hope to confess or repent your sins, if you don't know what sins you have committed that require confession?

It seems obvious, but it's easy, and common, to gloss over this stage. Many come to confession with a fuzzy and general sense of conviction for having done … something. Similarly, many of us who are white, come to confront our participation in racism with only a vague and amorphous feeling of white guilt. There are many reasons white guilt is unproductive, but it's aimlessness and imprecision is high on the list.

If we hope to change, if we hope to offer restitution, we must know, with specificity, and precision what harms we've committed or participated in. The process of uncovering and identifying these is layered, and might necessarily move in several directions at once.

Digging into the past and uncovering the present realities of our communities is the difficult process of recognizing and coming to terms with the mythologies we've been taught, and learning the real truth of our communities, which is often messier, more uncomfortable, and more interesting than the fairy tales handed down to us. Even our most basic assumptions regarding the position of our churches in their communities and neighborhoods may be called into question as we begin the work of fact-finding. Maggiano said this about his own congregation's learning process.

> *Baltimore is a very small, interconnected city and many of our churches are either in suburban enclaves or urban churches that people commute to on Sundays and then leave when they're done. So it's easier to be disconnected from your surroundings.*

Maggiano described how the economic landscape of Baltimore contributes to this trend of disengagement. The city is shaped by profound inequalities and segregation, where property values often plummet from one block to the next. Memorial, Maggiano noticed, sits in a middle-class enclave, surrounded by neighborhoods that are struggling.

> *We began to do a lot of work with St Catherine's of Alexandria, a Black Episcopal church, eight blocks from Memorial. We did some joint services, but the first major activity we did together outside of church was a mandated anti-racism retreat for church leadership. It was this powerful moment for Memorial, because you had this large group of women, who had been members of St. Catherine's for forty, fifty, sixty years. and they had never heard of Memorial. They didn't know anything about us. And Memorial thinks of itself as this amazing, wonderful place; that it's done all this great stuff. But here's a church eight blocks away, that doesn't know us from Adam.*
>
> *That was important. It showed, not just me, but it showed the whole church, how poorly we were doing in establishing good relationship.*

Those first steps in fact-finding will often be jarring and unsettling. Because we're confronted with the reality that who we think we are, and who we actually are, might not match. We may wonder if we need a profound shift in identity to bring them into alignment.

> *This is not a project of Memorial. This is a reorienting. It's about who we are as a community for the long term.*

That "long term" can be tough to wrestle with. Maggiano described how a priest called him from a church in a large Southern city. And he recognized that he had to do something around reparations. According to Maggiano:

> *His first question was, what can I do to make this racism stuff go away, so we can get back to the Gospel? But the problem is, dismantling racism is the Gospel. We've been ignoring it for years. Now we have to deal with it.*

Dealing with it, begins with uncovering the truth. Alongside intentional conversations with the surrounding neighborhood. Historical research can be essential. It is startling how quickly information about the past fades, or is glossed over.

Our Task Force's historian, Franklin A. Robinson Jr., is an archivist with the Smithsonian Museum of American History. He researched, wrote, and published "Faith & Tobacco: A History of St. Thomas' Episcopal Parish, Prince George's County, Maryland," an account of his home congregation's involvement in the tobacco economy of colonial Maryland. Robinson notes that

> *Much of what we lift up as congregational history is shown, upon closer investigation, to be mythology, built, perhaps, around a kernel of truth, but elaborated on, and redacted through multiple tellings, until the meaning of events is changed entirely.*

Robinson thinks that his interest in St. Thomas' history stems from the fact that he grew up in the parish. His family had been part of the church from the 1600s. During his youth, there were these myths about the parish: that a colonial rector descended from English nobility. Or, that another rector founded a school for African-Americans. When they celebrated the 250th anniversary of their church building in 1995, a building that was probably built, in part, by enslaved people, he decided to discover the truth behind these stories, writing a monograph for the 250th anniversary.

> *After that research into parish history, I focused on a broader question. I decided that what really interested me was how the tobacco economy supported the Church of England in Maryland in the colonial era. That gave the question and research some focus. And, in researching some of these myths, I found out the truth, as is usual, was more interesting than the myths we'd been fed.*

This is especially true where our history with white supremacy is concerned. Like most people, Episcopalians like to imagine our forebears heroically and righteously. With regard to race, this tendency means we'll often downplay our communities' history of racist practice, while exaggerating their moments of anti-racist endeavors. I've heard almost a dozen Episcopal congregations claim to have been stops on the underground railroad. Only two that I'm acquainted with actually took the time to research those claims. In both cases they proved false.

Robinson began this research as an amateur. His process of uncovering the congregation's story proves you don't have to be a trained historian to get started in this work.

You only have to be curious, methodical, and resourceful, because a lot of times you will have to dig. The biggest part of the word "research" is "search," and that's the key. You start with one thing, one question of your Church's history. That initial question will automatically lead to another, and another, and you just follow that trail until it ends.

Robinson says that the most important thing is not to be daunted by the task, to take it in small bites. For him,

It's the best detective novel ever, because you're always looking for clues to lead you back to the truth.

If you want to learn about your congregation's involvement with slavery, if you have a passion for it, and are interested, you can do it.

It may be that your church doesn't have a direct connection to slavery. But in this country, wherever you are, there is a story to learn about how racism and race has shaped your community. For churches and other religious institutions you can start by asking: What does our community look like? Who worships with us? Who doesn't? Do our demographics match the neighborhood around us? How did this come about? How and why was our community founded? Where did the first members come from? Who funded your community in its early days? Where did those funds come from?

Start with one question and follow it as far as you can go, other questions will arise naturally as you search. Church records and municipal archives can be treasure troves of information. Follow the paper trail; follow the money. Ask yourself what's not being said. Be ready to question fundamental assumptions you may have about your congregation and community, and learn to be unsatisfied with easy answers.

Memorial found their way toward making their rather extraordinary reparations commitment, in large part because of their willingness to continue asking honest, difficult questions about their own community. As Maggiano tells it:

> *I came to Memorial six years ago and came in knowing that it was a church that had had, previously, a glory period: a long period of success focused around a lot of justice related issues. And it was also a church that had been through some extraordinarily difficult times in the more recent past. When I came to Memorial, they described themselves as seeking diversity but not having it, which I thought was honest. Coming to Baltimore, post Freddie Gray, was a unique opportunity to learn what ministry is like in a hyper-segregated city that is seeking to be better.*

Maggiano admits that there were things he didn't know. He tried to recognize his own limitations in terms of ministry. And he wanted the church to recognize its limitations, what it didn't know, especially around the issues of race.

> *The first thing that we did when I got there was just some story-telling about who we were. We interviewed as many people as we could in the parish about their connection with justice, how they understood what social justice involved.*

The results were interesting and enlightening. Maggiano got to see people's memories of the period before his predecessor. He heard stories about actions they'd taken on justice issues related to Freddie Gray's death, and about justice work around women's ordination.

> *But it happened in the context of this very white church in the midst of a very Black city. So I innocently asked the question, "Why is that?"*

At first the response was what you always hear, "It's just geography," or whatever.

But when he dug a little bit deeper, he discovered that the stories the church had told itself about itself, especially from that period in the forties, fifties, sixties, were largely not true. That it was in fact, an explicitly segregated congregation and worked hard to keep it that way. They fired a priest, who tried to integrate the church. Maggiano suspects this might explain why the church had a continued disconnection from Black Baltimore.

In the EDOW, we've delegated the archival work of truth-finding to Robinson. We circumscribed his work to one question: What was the involvement of Diocesan antecedents (the congregations and other institutions that came to form the Diocese of Washington), in chattel slavery?

In pursuing this research, we found it important to acknowledge, and be aware of the broad scope of racist harms, while keeping the focus of our truth-finding bounded. The scope of racist harms is wide: it includes not only harms to the Black community, but land theft and genocide committed against Indigenous Americans, and systemic discrimination against Latinos and Asians.

Likewise, racist harms inflicted on the Black community did not end with emancipation, but continued through de jure and de facto segregation, mass incarceration, displacement and gentrification.

To ignore this breadth would be to participate in another kind of erasure. At the same time, it's necessary to put boundaries around the questions, so we have a place to begin, and clear goals we can measure. Furthermore, if we fail to be specific in our questions, if we make our inquiry too broad, we will end up diluting, and muddling the histories of the many distinct communities owed reparations. So we focus our investigation and goals on one community—Black descendants of enslaved people—and one question: how did our diocese benefit from chattel slavery? We do this knowing and acknowledging that answering this one question will mean only that we have taken the first step along our path.

Even when you set the close boundaries around your questions, you may be surprised by the winding paths they take you on. The story of racist theft and plunder is a complicated one, and rarely follows a straight line. Imani lays out some of the myriad, surprising and complicated ways that history of racist exploitation shows up, and still plays out today:

> *Think for a minute about the slave trade. It's got multiple dimensions. A lot of people just think about stolen labor. We think about being snatched from your homeland and detached from your culture. We think about being forced to work to work the land. We think about plantation slavery in a rural agricultural context.*

For many, this framing serves to protect us. It puts a neat hedge between our current realities, which might be, for instance, Northern, urban, modern, or industrial, and the narrow chattel slavery of our imagination: strictly Southern, rural, antebellum and rural. Imani invites us to look further, to consider the myriad ways slavery developed, and its ongoing impact on our lives today.

> *If we look to New England, we find industries in Baltimore or Maine, like the fish oil industry, where enslaved people are doing that fishing, and enslaved people are harvesting the oil. Enslaved people are building all of these industries,*

These Northern, slave-driven industries shaped the landscape and provided capital for the growth of cities, factories and bedroom communities throughout New England. And Imani points out how the weight of slavery extends, even beyond the East Coast.

> *The entire insurance industry that rises around enslavement. There are people who make their money speculating on, and insuring, the value of Black bodies. There's a complicated, fully three-dimensional, legally sanctioned, economy built up on the backs of stolen human beings. The impact of that is deep.*

The whole finance sector, which undergirds and drives so much of our economy is built, at least in part, on capitol amassed through slavery. Whether directly, or indirectly, our church pensions, endowments, insurance policies and mortgages sit on a foundation mixed with the sweat and blood of enslaved people. In more concrete terms, many of our congregations and other public institutions were built, literally, by enslaved hands.

> *Up through the Civil War you see enslaved people building up colleges, and buildings, and government offices, even the Capitol Building. And all the way through that, their families are continually dehumanized, in and out of the system.*

The legacy of slavery extends far beyond physical and financial capital, into the social institutions that hold our republic together.

> *There are enslaved people, enslaved soldiers, fighting in battles throughout the revolutionary war. Without them, the war isn't won. Without them this nation doesn't exist.*

And that legacy doesn't end with emancipation, but continues forward right into our contemporary moment, showing up in surprising ways and places. The *New York Times* "1619 Project" offer an omnibus of the peculiar imprints of slavery and exploited Black labor on contemporary society, everything from our cities traffic patterns to our nation's oversweetened palates. Imani shared another relic, which was news to me:

> *After the war, we can track how all these industries, and infrastructure, and homes, are still built with exploited Black labor. That still shapes policy today. Think about the role of H-2 Visa workers, the folks with temporary work visas. That program was utilized to bring in low-wage Black laborers for Florida's sugar economy. Now, in the contemporary context, we have H-2 Visa workers who are doing these high-intensity, under-paid, jobs that sustain our economy.*

And all of this *catalogs* only the legally sanctioned abuses. All the way through enslavers and slave traders we busy circumventing, or flagrantly ignoring even those minimal restrictions the federal government had imposed on the institution of chattel slavery.

> *The law banning international importation of slaves goes into effect in 1808. But people are still smuggled, trafficked, and put through the agony of the middle passage. And there's an industry behind all that. You have to pay a certain cost per weight and volume to transport cargo, no matter what the cargo is. So you packed people in, stacked them like boxes, to make maximum profit.*

And this is more than just a litany of historical wrongs. The impact of these myriad manifestations of slavery extend into the present day, and still operate to impoverish and disadvantage the Black community:

Consider all the promises made and broken: the general order for the distribution of land, and the constitutional amendments to secure our rights. Those are all promises that get broken. Again and again you see the exploitation of Black time, labor, and resources. Historically, whenever Black are able to amass a little bit of something, either domestic terrorism destroys it or other people con them out of it—often legally.

That tale of terrorism, theft and grift, is precisely the history we must search out, uncover, name, and publicize. Here in the Diocese of Washington, we can trace part of that stream of wealth that was stolen, and piled up, through our involvement with slavery. The path is indirect but evident.

Robinson describes how in Maryland the church was supported through a tobacco tax. It was set at forty pounds of tobacco per poll with the passage of the Establishment Act in 1692. Taxable persons, a "poll," included all white males sixteen and over and all black males and females sixteen and over. Taxable white males over 16 who owned enslaved paid the forty pounds of tobacco per poll for each of their enslaved sixteen and over. The tobacco taxes they enacted went directly to support the priests in established parishes,

That's how they were funded. Building of churches, upkeep of graveyards and the like took an act of Assembly to levy additional tobacco taxes for those expenses. Tobacco was the commodity funding that tax, and, in whole or in part, enslaved laborers were used to make the crop of tobacco. The tobacco tax is the unique tie to enslavement that the Church of England in Maryland, which later became the Protestant Episcopal Church, bore.

This unique and peculiar tie to enslavement is instructive precisely because it is indirect and obscure. When we imagine and look for the traces of slavery and anti-Black racism, we tend to seek out most direct examples. These overt manifestations are easier to uncover and identify. They naturally draw our attention. But, like a stage magician's legerdemain, they may draw our attention away from other, covert and indirect legacies of harm. After all, as Robinson notes:

> The Church of England connection to enslavement is not as much in your face, say, as the Jesuit connection where there was no hesitancy about it. They enslaved people, they bought them, sold them, they had them work their plantations in Newtown Neck in St. Mary's County, where there's a lot of archeology going on right now. That is where a group of enslaved people were sold south by the Jesuits to fund Georgetown University. Our experience is different. I still have not found a Maryland parish that actually engaged in the slave trade in a primary way, i.e., buying and selling on behalf of the parish on a regular basis.

When Robinson shared this information with the Task Force, that none of Maryland congregations, as congregations, had enslaved people, there was an audible sigh of relief in the room, as if we had somehow dodged history's bullet. As we research and uncover the past, this hope, to find absolution in the historical record, will tempt almost all of us. We should be skeptical of it. If we are too hasty to pronounce our own acquittal, there's a good chance we're overlooking our own, more obscure connections to the history anti-Black racism. And sometimes, these connections are not all that obscure. Robinson reminded us:

> Of course, we had parish leaders who did engage in the slave trade, were enslavers. There was always a certain percentage of them participating in enslavement.

In fact, in the time since our first interview, Robinson has uncovered evidence of at least one Maryland parish that did profit directly from the sale of enslaver persons. As you learn and uncover these stories, especially if you are looking back to the period of chattel slavery, you may find yourself imagining this as a tale of times long past. It is not. Imani, recalled a moment that underscored the nearness of this history:

> *I heard an interview on CBS Sunday Morning with a Black man whose great-grandfather was in the crowd in Galveston when the first Juneteenth was announced. And he mentioned that when he talked to one of his older cousins about this ancestor, they said, "Yeah, I knew him." It's very recent.*

For me, Imani's comment brought to mind a time two years ago, when Zora Neale Hurston's book *Barracoon* was finally released. It tells the story of Cudjo Lewis, one of the last survivors of the middle passage, illegally smuggled after the international slave trade was banned. He died in 1935. Just after I read it, I had a pastoral call with a member of my congregation who was a hundred and two. She was telling a story about her high school, Dunbar. And I remember thinking: *When you were in high school, there were still survivors of the middle passage walking this Earth. And now, you and I are talking on the phone right now, in 2020.* We must remember, here in the United States, this is all recent history.

Historical research, digging through archives and records is essential. There are parts of the story that can only be found in the paperwork. But archives and records alone won't tell the fullness of the story. We need to listen to the stories of the hurt directly from those who know it. We need to make space to hear their stories of these uncomfortable truths in their own voices.

In the EDOW, our Accountability Board pushed this point forward, asking the Task Force to host listening sessions, where those who've been impacted by overtly or covertly racist policies of the diocese would be given space to speak and be heard.

This is vitally important work. It's also extremely delicate. These sort of listening sessions amount to asking people who may be traumatized, to make themselves vulnerable, return to their trauma, and share it, in a venue and with an audience, where they can't be certain of the response. Listening sessions are dangerous, by definition. But they are the only place certain truths can be heard.

Our Advisory Board exhorted us to lay the groundwork to create as safe a space as possible for those who would be sharing their stories. This meant establishing a baseline of consensus around the reality that racist harms had been committed, so the basic plausibility of the stories being shared wouldn't be unfairly questioned. It meant educating ourselves, our congregations and members in the basic concepts and terms of reparations and white supremacist harm, so our truth-tellers wouldn't be obliged to do remedial work.

We worked toward these first two goals with a series of online presentations to the diocese, a two-week parochial adult-education curriculum, a day long Diocesan-wide symposium, and a whole lot of conversations. This preparatory work takes time. No one said truth-finding was easy. But it's necessary if we hope to make our way toward repair.

Our attitude as we encounter these uncomfortable questions, and equally uncomfortable answers, must be one of openness and curiosity. And it is tough to maintain, especially when the questions seem to touch us personally. Fisher-Stewart has a skill for posing the questions everyone else wants to ignore. As she and I talked about this work, she asked:

I have noticed that a lot of these Black women, who are called as Bishops to these white, white dioceses, can't get any whiter, are in interracial marriages. I was wondering, did they choose these Bishops because your white husband or your white wife made them feel a little more comfortable? These are the types of questions we need to ask, the ones that are necessary to get a diagnosis. And we have to ask them, knowing that you may well get crickets. That's tough for us to do. But at least the question is out there.

This question, in particular, made me squirm. In part because I personally know, and respect, several of the bishops she is talking about. But in part because I am a white man, married to a Black clergywoman in the Episcopal Church. The question cut close to home. I felt tempted to shut down. That feeling, that pull to disengage, should be our cue to look more closely. We need to notice the patterns of race we want to ignore, and then ask the question, "Why?" Why do our congregations look the way we do? What do the racial patterns in our leadership mean?

As we learn truths that may be painful, uncomfortable and outside experience, it's important to meet them with a spirit of principled empathy. We must be empathetic in striving to imagine, as far as is possible, what the truths we are learning would mean for those who experienced them. We must be principled in recognizing that our imaginations are just that: imagination.

It can be tempting to overestimate our own understanding, or the relevance of our own experience. If you are, for instance, a woman, or queer, or disabled, you might assume your experience of various systems of oppression give you special insight into the harms of racism. This can be a dangerous trap.

Ayers noted that, even as a Black person, she needed to mind the distance between her own experience of racism, and that of the community she was working to learn from:

> *I live in Northeast, over in Ivy City. Whenever an Uber driver drops me off over here, they say, "Well, this didn't look like this before." And I always wonder: Well, what did it look like? What neighborhood did I just land in? Am I a gentrifier? Have I done something wrong? It was all warehouses before. Now it's got a Target and an organic grocery store.*
>
> *While I can relate on some level, being a descendant of slaves and being Black, it is not the same as being a Black Washingtonian, who has lived through some wild times. And I'm thinking: This is not an experience I had. I wasn't here when crack was on the streets and people were experiencing high levels of addiction en masse. So when I visit homeless shelters and speak with older Black men, and they tell me about those times, I shut up and listen.*

The way Ayers responds to these questions demonstrates what I mean by "principled empathy." She doesn't not shy away from the distance between her own experience and that of the community she's working with. She doesn't chase after false analogies to her own experience. Instead, she pulls on those parts of her own identity that motivate her to reach out with genuine curiosity. This allows her to show up authentically as herself, without re-centering her own experience. In particular she draws on her experience of growing up as an army brat, moving around without any fixed hometown:

> *Not having the experience of home makes me curious about what home means to other people, and how they perceive their home, and how they perceive people that are not from their*

home. I've never felt like an outsider, but have felt like a guest. As a Southerner, I take being a guest very seriously. I never want to be in someone's home with my shoes on when they've asked her to take them off. I always put first that this is your home. If I think that I know more than you about your home, I'm not helpful to you at all. I'm only helpful if I've heard you; if I've seen you; if I've made my best effort to understand you, and if I'm centering your demands and requests in the conversation.

This skill, of claiming and engaging the parts of our own stories that draw our attention past our own stories, is crucial in the work of truth-finding. But ultimately, the best remedy and the best protection against this temptation to overestimate our own understanding and comprehension is to keep leaning into relationship: to broaden and deepen our engagement with the directly impacted communities around us.

The last temptation we will face in this work of truth-finding, is the temptation to prematurely close the book, to decide, arbitrarily, that we've learned the whole story, and that there is no more to discover. With five hundred years of white supremacist history behind us, the path of harms trails back far and wide. We may never know the whole story in our lives, so we must commit to a process of continual uncovering. As Ayers notes, grounding the work in curiosity is essential:

The best way to go about doing this work is to start with questions. A lot of questions. Questions give us more answers than answers can themselves. And the first question to ask is why are we here? Why do you want to undertake reparations? If you want to do reparations work like everybody else, then go back to the drawing board. That's not the best reason. You won't solve anything if your heart's not in it.

That question, the question of why you're doing this, is one of the most difficult to wrestle with. If, like me, you're convinced that reparations are a moral imperative, you'd probably answer "it's the right thing to do." But, while I do generally believe there's no wrong reason for doing the right thing, "because we're supposed to," is likely too weak a response to carry us through to the end of the work. This journey is not a short one.

> *"What did we do wrong? What are the harms we took part in?"*
> *As I've begun to consider this work on a national scale, I've seen how that question can be a bit of a rabbit hole: each harm you uncover leads to another. But you have to excavate that history.*
> *That can be scary and disheartening, because you start to feel like there may be no end to the research. And yes, it's worthy of great lament. But if you can find your way to still being curious, as curious as you can be, you can go down those rabbit holes, and face it, for what it really is. As long as you stay at the surface level, the source of the rot is going to bear its fruit.*
> *That's a biblical principle. You have to pluck it up at the root. If you leave the root it'll keep bearing fruit. And you'll just keep cutting off rotten fruit. You've got to look at these racialized harms and ask, "How did we get here?"*

That last question may be the most important question you can ask. White supremacy shapes and pervades our world so deeply, and has done so for so long that many times we're conditioned to assume its results are natural or inevitable. Fisher-Stewart calls the question as she looks at the racial demographics of our congregations:

> *We don't have a diagnosis and getting a diagnosis would actually take a different kind of survey of all of the parishes. We'd have*

to go in and ask why are you so white? Why are you so Black?
Why did you establish a separate Black congregation? Or a sepa-
rate Latino one? But we don't ask those questions in a really deep
way. We just say, "Oh, they wanted to be on their own, so we put
them over there."

This is part of how white supremacy sustains itself: by con-
vincing us it's just the way things are. Wherever and whenever
we notice racial inequities and divisions in our institutions we
need to ask, "How did this happen? How did we get here?" And
we must learn to interrogate the easy and comfortable answers.
There's a kind of strong-willed humility that's required here.
Ayers counsels anyone considering the work:

In that spirit of humility, the most important question you have
to keep asking is "What don't we know?" That's something they
teach in law school. Figure out what you don't know immedi-
ately. And figure out what you don't know you don't know. Keep
asking, "What am I missing here?"

5

Truth-Telling

Once the truth of harms inflicted is known, it must be told. This is the process of public confession. It occur in multiple interactions, both inside and outside the institution, and in multiple mediums. Our nation, and our churches, have spent generations covering over the history of racist harms with myths, half-truths, rationalizations, professed ignorance, erasure and outright lies. Acknowledging and owning the truth will not be a one and done affair. We will return to it many times, to truly come to terms with it.

It must be shared in many venues and formats. In the EDOW, we have taught the truth of our history with congregational adult education curriculums, YouTube videos, public symposiums, formal resolutions and press releases. In this breadth and diversity of truth-telling we are attempting to banish the lies that have captured our collective imagination regarding our history with racism and race. That work must be pursued persistently. And it must be pursued properly. The way we tell the truth, and which truths we choose to tell, can make all the difference between a genuine apology carrying the potential for transformative change, and a tired platitude that only reinforces old patterns of hurt. Imani describes the kind of intentionality proper truth-telling requires:

I was working with an organization that was meeting about Juneteenth celebrations and the team wanted to do some kind of social media post. But it was just random. They wanted something highlighting Harriett Tubman's house, or something at Fredrick Douglass's place, that had no particular connection to the meaning of that day. There was no intentionality about it. They just wanted to do this smorgasbord of Blackness. That doesn't respect us, or our history. Of course that wasn't the intent, but that was the effect of utilizing Juneteenth to highlight anything Black.

Juneteenth has a particular meaning, connected to a particular time, and a particular place in Texas. That has to be respected. So I told them, no, we're not doing it like that. We can do it later when we've had time to think about it intentionally. Making time and space to do things with the proper intention is part of how I try to respond compassionately.

It might feel tempting to file this example under the innocuous heading "well-intentioned but misguided." But we must understand that all our efforts at truth-telling about racism will happen in the context of four hundred years of paternalism, broken promises and doublespeak. If we are not deeply intentional, we will end up doing further harm. Imani describes that experience viscerally:

I live in a Black woman's body all day, every day. So whether it's people in the store looking at me suspiciously, wondering if I'm going to steal something, or people talking to me like I'm not a human being, or asking myself if I'll get proper care when I go in for basic medical services, or the cashier going out his way to not touch my hand when giving me change, we put up with constant microaggressions every day. Those of us subjected to white supremacy as targets of its violence get so inflamed by its daily, and I mean daily, impact that it doesn't take much to piss us off. We're raw from it.

So we must proceed carefully, and attentively. Confession and truth-telling are akin to making an apology, and follow many of the same rules. Your institution's confession should be clear, specific, and as brief as possible while conveying all necessary information. Long-winded statements of regret are generally more for the benefit of the one confessing than for the one who has been harmed. Your confession should focus on the actions of your institution, both historical and contemporary, and the ways they may have inflicted harm. There is power in the speaking of the simple, unadorned truth. Again, Imani shares what that power looks like:

> *It comes through that scriptural precedent: "You shall know the truth, and the truth shall make you free." I like that particular translation of it: not that the truth will set you free, but that the truth will make you free. That's why I don't sensationalize the truth. I don't. I just tell it. And I repeat it often. Because truth has power. That's why there's so much contest over what gets taught in our schools.*

We've all heard how that contest and debate echoes through our world today. It sometimes seems truth is under siege. If we are to engage in the work of truth-telling, we must be prepared to experience resistance. As Imani notes, the resistance itself, that contest, is a recognition and response to the power of the truths we are sharing. The corollary is that, if our truth-telling does not provoke response, reaction and even resistance, then it is likely we've stayed at the superficial level; that we haven't dug deep into the uncomfortable, powerful, and transformative truths of our shared history. If things are going too smoothly, it may be time to return to your relationships of accountability and ask, "Are we sugarcoating this? Are there more stories we need to hear and tell?"

The act of truth-telling is a long-haul endeavor. As any educator will tell you, teaching is about repetition. We can't just say it once, or twice, and expect to be heard. We can't publish a single, grand, history of our institution's history with race and racism, and expect the work to be done. Telling the truth takes time, and perseverance. So we need to go in with the spiritual resources necessary to endure. Imani talks about what keeps her going.

> *That struggle, that contest, can be draining. That's why you need the faith component. We have to trust that God will fulfill God's promises to us. We have to trust that if we jump out there, and if we tell the truth, then we'll get a return on it. But you can't get too invested in the outcome. Not that you don't care about the outcome, because you do care. But if you get so consumed, where your ego is thirsty to see this one outcome, to see it exactly the way you wanted it, in your own time, that's going to be a problem.*

Again, taking a cue from the norms of a proper apology, it's important to distinguish between the harms your institution has inflicted, for which you can, and should take responsibility, and the emotional response of the people directly impacted by those harms, which is theirs and theirs alone. You cannot claim it. Apologizing for, or making excuses for, other people's feelings veers easily into blaming the victim. This distinction may seem subtle, but we can understand it easily enough if we remember the difference between hearing someone tell you, "I'm sorry you were offended," which implicitly blames the victim for being offended, and hearing someone say, "I'm sorry I hurt you," which solely expresses the aggressor's contrition for the things they have done.

Taking personal responsibility is essential. It can be very tempting, especially when dealing with historical injuries, to separate ourselves from the offense, to say that this is something someone else did, long ago. It's important to locate our own relationship to the offense. Ayers shows how to trace the connection:

> *I think the biggest danger facing us as it relates to reparations is people saying, "That it's not our problem." I've heard that quite a bit, especially from people my age, in their early thirties. They say, "This is not our problem. We don't have those problems."*
>
> *But it's everybody's problem. We live in a country that is fundamentally based on racism. This country was founded with Black people being told they are less than, and are only worthy of being owned by white people. That's baked into our foundation. I don't care how many people want to ban Critical Race theory. These are just the facts. This is the history. And it is very dangerous to pretend we're past it.*

As you frame your institutional confession, remove any, and all statements in the passive voice. Be clear about who did what. Avoid conditional declarations, things like "harms we may have inflicted." Check every use of the word "if," and be sure it is actually necessary. This is not a time to be mealy mouthed.

Avoid all attempts at rationalization, or down-playing uncomfortable history as "a product of its time." State the facts and own them. Most importantly, you should be ready and able to identify the connections between past histories of racist abuse, and the current situation of your church or institution. How did it shape the way your community looks today? Were assets gained through these abuses? If so, where are they now? Where can the effects of these hurts be seen today? Where are they still taking place? Answer these questions, and back it up with receipts. As Robinson advises:

I've come to value action based on truth-telling. A lot of people jump into the argument from a position of personal mythology or the mythology that's taken for granted in the community. I always think it's better if we can say, "Let's take a breath. Let's look at the historical record. Let's base how we choose to go forward, based on the facts and what we know, as opposed to what we suppose and think we know."

As we say in every confession, acknowledge the sins you have committed, things you have done, and things you have left undone: the places your institution has turned a blind eye to injustice, sat comfortably with the racism of its own structures, and quietly made peace with oppression. This matters too. But again, be as specific as you are able.

Fisher-Stewart put her finger on the need for that specificity, and the need to wrestle, collectively, with the truth, until we can name it with precision.

White people have to enunciate what they are repairing, and then have Black people agree to it. We're not going to tell you what it is. You have to start. What is it you think is broken? What has the church, this church that is grounded in whiteness, a majority white church, done? How has it broken the relationship with Black people? When whites can finally say, "This is the harm done, this is what the church has done," and list it out, then we can start talking about how to repair.

The listing, the specificity, that Fisher-Stewart calls for, is precisely what has been missing from so many of our institutional statements or repentance for racism. And it may be why these statements have so often produced such disappointing and frustrating results. Fisher-Stewart continues:

In 2006, the Episcopal Church apologized for slavery. And there have been iterations of this apology. But they just keep saying we apologize for slavery. What's missing are the questions, "What specifically are you apologizing for? What has the church's involvement in slavery done? Intergenerationally historically, how do we see that still manifesting itself today?" Because when you say slavery, that stops at 1865. And there's a big gap between then and now. We want to skip over the specific harms and put the band-aid of reparations on it. And then it becomes just a bribe to forget the past, forget the harm.

To really have the discussion about reparations, white people need to dig into that question of the ongoing harm from 1619 to now. And we'll listen, we'll nudge you, but we're not going to give you the answer. You're going to have to work through that for yourselves.

6

Repentance

I n my youth, like many teenagers, I made a big show of "being responsible." From age fourteen to eighteen, "I'll take care of that," were my by-words. But I was weak on follow through, with the result that I made, and broke, a great many promises. At which point I would apologize. And then I would do it again. The pattern only changed when my sister Maria confronted me, after one particular broken promise had left her up a creek without a paddle. I don't remember the details, but I do remember her rebuke: "Don't say 'I'm sorry.' It's meaningless when you say it."

Confession without repentance is only empty words. Confession without repentance is equivalent to offering repeated apology without changing the behavior that caused offense. And it is every bit as galling and dooming in relationship. It has also been precisely the pattern of predominantly white institutions in confronting our own racist histories. In recent years white congregations, white dioceses/synods, and white denominations have issued reams of resolutions and public statements acknowledging a history of participation in white supremacy. These statements have not, in the main, led to any substantial changes to the white supremacists practices of our denominations. As Angie Shannon noted regarding the Evangelical Lutheran Church in America (ELCA): "We are wildly confessional, but minimally repentant." We must do better.

Etymology and biblical linguistics aside, many preachers will tell you repentance means turning around, changing
direction, doing something different. I believe this is the cor-
rect understanding of how Jesus uses the word. This is why
he speaks of "bearing fruit worthy of repentance." Repentance
means changing what we're doing now, so we achieve different,
more godly, results in the future. Robinson shares his own story
of the path from learning, and speaking the truths of the past
toward change and repentance:

> *Was it a Damascus Road moment? No. I think you have to know
> your history in order to move forward and especially in our work,
> this reparations work. In the work I did with my parish, I came
> to a point where I had to confront, and accept the responsibility
> of our history, even though we were not the ones who enslaved
> anybody. We can say, "Well they didn't know any better." But
> that economic engine of enslavement was still moving through
> our history. You can say,. "That's just what everybody did." But
> again, that economic engine of enslavement was still moving
> through our history. No matter what argument you choose, yes,
> benefited from enslavement both directly and indirectly. So you
> say: Let's repair this, let's fix this. Let's step up to the plate.*

"Stepping up to the plate," requires a certain degree of grit.
For the work of reparations to have integrity and endurance,
you will need to commit to the personal, internal, work of
repentance.

Schulken walks the walk of repenting from whiteness better perhaps than any other white person I've met. For her, that
integrity comes by way of personal relationship. Her adopted
daughter is Korean, and Schulken's determined to manage
the fraught racial dynamics of that space responsibly. It's not
always easy:

For white people, we can get lost if we haven't taken some time to do the work ourselves, if we haven't taken the time to really examine our beliefs, if we haven't taken the time trying to look at the world through the eyes of folks who are not white.

I've done as much reading as I can about how whiteness works. It started with my daughter when I realized I needed to understand what it's going to be like for her to be Asian in this country.

This internal work of repentance is essential, but can easily turn to navel-gazing if we don't act on what we've learned in the community beyond ourselves. If you're white, one of the most obvious places to begin is by inviting other white folks into the work of personal repentance, something Schulken has done quite a bit.

As I've learned what that's like, I've tried to share it with others. One time in our adoptive parent discussion groups, an adoptive mom came to her and said, "My husband's really excited about all those resources you shared several years ago, like the Angry Asian Man blog, and he keeps referring to them and learning from them.

Like Schulken, my own motivation comes through personal relationships. The harms of anti-Black racism land directly on my wife, my son, my extended family and circle of friends, and the congregation I serve and have come to love. As Schulken once mentioned to me, if you don't have these relationships in your life, I can't say what would motivate you to take this on. But you will need to find that motivation regardless. And you'll need to hold it tight. Because the work of repentance is humbling, and it will make you want to quit. It's work of seeking out your ignorance, limitations, and misunderstanding, and facing them all directly. Schulken describes it like this:

The reality is, white people are so blind, and unless we acknowledge that, and work on that, we're just going to keep causing problems. That's the first piece of work we've got to do. We talk about being "woke," but it's actually about waking up. We're not awake. We're unwoke, and we're in the process of waking up from whiteness.

Schulken describes how, in the adoption community, adult adoptees often use the term "coming out of the fog" to describe what it's like realizing that so many of the stories they were told about their adoption and adoption in general are fairy tales.

She suggests the same thing applies to white folks working on race, and notes that it's a humbling process, like having your blinders removed. This can be a very, very uncomfortable feeling. She's noticed that so much of the way we talk about race in this country is really about keeping white people comfortable.

As you start to get at the truth, you have to put your comfort aside. As I started to get at the truth of my own upbringing, my own feelings, and the things I was taught, I kept thinking, "but I'm a good, liberal, progressive, open-minded person." I had to put that aside. As I keep reading, and talking with folks, and taking classes, I keep finding these blind spots. Each time I find one, I think, "Okay I need to work on that." That's just part of repentance and confession. The full meaning of repentance, not just to feel regret, but to turn around and go in a new direction. Like we say each Sunday, we confess "things done, and left undone."

Personal repentance is essential, but ultimately, durable change comes by way of institutional repentance. Institutionally, repentance means changing policy, leadership, and the structures of governance. It means recognizing that the institution, in this case the church as currently shaped has consistently produced, and reproduced, racially unjust outcomes. If we hope for the church to produce fruits worthy of repentance, fruits of justice, we must go to the root, and change the way we do things from the ground up. The measure of this change will not be the words we speak, or the commitments we profess. It will be the results we produce. Again, Jesus teaches us "by their fruits you shall know them." Ibram X. Kendi, author of *Stamped from the Beginning: The Definitive History of Racist Ideas In America*, teaches that policy which produces racially inequitable outcomes is, by definition, racist, while policy which increases racial equity is, by definition, anti-racist, and that these are the only two options given to us. I suspect Jesus likes the way Kendi thinks.

If the measure of our repentance are the fruits it bears, that is, the outcomes that follow, then our commitment to repentance should be formulated with an eye toward results. We need to set measurable goals: clearly stated racial representation objectives in each tier of leadership, equitable hiring targets, representational allocation of resources, and more. We need to set clear timelines for reaching these goals, and we need to establish structures of accountability that will hold us to our objectives. In general, this will require recruiting outside partners who will audit our efforts, and don't mind challenging us. We're not looking to be made comfortable; we're trying to be the church Christ calls us to be.

While institutional repentance must be measurable, and subject to accounting, in order to have any true meaning, it is, ultimately, a spiritual process, one that seeks to transform hearts and minds, as well as structures they support. As in all stages of the reparations process, that work occurs in relationship. Ayers offers a model of how to begin:

*Any group should be talking to their own group about the issues.
Like I tell men, talk to your homeboys, they're doing things that
are not cool to women. I say the same thing to my white friends.
They've asked me, "Lindsay, how do I show up for you in this
space?" I say, "You need to go back to your hometown and talk to
your mom if she doesn't understand, or your dad, or your sister."
We often think our justice work has to be this grandiose Insta-
gram-worthy thing. But a lot of it happens around the kitchen
table. That might be a biblical perspective of mine, or maybe a
Southern one.*

*Have those conversations at the table. Be mindful of when
those conversations are happening in an unhealthy way and
speak up. Show up and keep supporting the work. Because it is
a polarizing issue. People have varying opinions on what reparation should look like or if it should even exist at all. If white
people just continue to engage in dialogue, with Black people as
well, we can actually move the needle on this quite a bit.*

It will, necessarily, be an ongoing process. We understand
this intuitively with regard to so many aspects of our Christian
life. No serious disciple expects to ever achieve the full fruits of
the spirit in this life. We will never be as honest, brave, faithful
or compassionate as we are called to be, in this life. But, by the
grace of God, we can strive to keep moving in that direction.
Repenting from patterns of racist harm is no different. We may
never reach a point where we have arrived and can say, "It is
done. We've rooted it all out." But we must strive to continue
moving in that direction, nonetheless. Maggiano and Memorial Church work to keep that attitude before them at all times:

*We've been pretty clear that this is not a project of Memorial.
This is a reorienting. It's about who we are as a community for
the long term. This is not a thing that we're going to do and then*

to do something else. We're going to be a Jesus centered, justice-fo-
cused community that works in relationship.

This doesn't preclude, or contradict the need to set clear, specific and measurable goals. Those kind of targets are essential for accountability and planning. But it does mean keeping perspective on what those goals, and their completion, actually represent. Maggiano describes his congregation's publicly stated goal this way:

People often ask, "How did you come up with half a million dol-
lars?" And honestly, it was a nice round number that seemed
achievable in five years. It doesn't mean that we're going to stop
when we hit that number, or even that we'd be a failure if we
didn't get there in five years. But it is going to be a continuing
and evolving part of our common life.

It's a process of ongoing formation around the Gospel. And
it's liberating. You get to work to create a community where this
is less of an issue for the next generation than it is for us. Versus
saying: "We're going to finish once and for all." Well, you won't be
able to do that.

Within our congregations and communities we will need to accept that being a repenting community, a community turning away from its history with white supremacy is now part of our mission and identity. At the individual level, this process of ongoing repentance can be daunting. But it can also be fulfilling. Schulken talks about the continual, ongoing internal process of repentance that accompanies this work:

White folks need to listen and read. They need to start by edu-
cating themselves as much as they can and really listening to the
experiences of other people. In this case, they need to listen to the
experience of people of color, not that of other white folks. It's hard

when you've been privileged. You're used to speaking up. You're used to taking up space

My daughter and I just returned from a Korean adoption conference in Colorado. It started out as a parent-run organization but it's now very much an adult-adoptee run organization, and they work intentionally to center the voices of adoptees.

At the conference, they conducted fish-bowl sessions. Schulken had never seen this done before. They placed adult adoptees in the center, speaking and leading the conversation, while the rest of the attendees were around the outside listening, not allowed to speak.

In the same way, in the work that we're doing, we need to center the voices of the people of color. We need to be quiet and let them speak.

Before white folks dive into this, they need to prepare themselves for it, prepare themselves to listen. They need to read, and take classes, and get educated. You have to be prepared for living into that for the rest of your life.

We also need to accept that we won't follow a path of linear progress. It will move in fits and starts, following surprising and winding courses. The important point is that we continue to move. Memorial went through many iterations of this work:

It was a process for us. We did some truth-telling and some confession. And then we took a break. And then we did more truth-telling and confession. And then we took a break. And then we did more truth-telling and confession. And then we took a break.

Along the way, they learned of a particular priest who'd led there for forty five years, from the 1880s until the 1920s.

He'd been a private in the Confederate army and continued to wear his Confederate uniform up and down the streets of Bolt Hill, in Baltimore, well until the day he died. Memorial was the church where the Confederate veterans and Sons of the Confederacy and Daughters of the Confederacy held meetings. That same priest inaugurated the Confederate monuments in Baltimore and advocated for segregation and disenfranchising Black voters.

As Maggiano and his church dug into the history of the founders of the church, they discovered that their first two priests who still had honorific plaques on the walls of the church, were enslavers. .

As Memorial continued their research, the question of their legacy with slavery shifted, unexpected, from the academic, to the personal. Memorial's deacon, Reverend Conway, had been researching her own family genealogy and learned that her family had been enslaved by the family of Charles Lee Howard, Memorial's founder. Her great grandmother was born the same year as Charles Lee Howard on the same plantation.

> *With that closeness of connection, the congregation was almost forced to say, "We've got to do something." And I know it's frustrating that the bar for white people to acknowledge historical realities is so high. Sometimes it seems like it will take forever for something to get done.*

Even more difficult than accepting the perpetually ongoing nature of institutional repentance is accepting the uncertainty of the repentance process. There is no finished plan for finding our way toward being a truly repentant church, because the church has never been one before. I asked Fisher-Stewart what she imagined the church would look like if we ever truly kicked the habit of white supremacy.

We don't know what the church looks like when it actually becomes inclusive. Maybe we should find out.

She recalled the church fathers and their church mothers, who left the church and went out to the desert, as if to say, "Let me leave this world behind because I'm done with it."

We could step out of these buildings of the church and leave it behind to become something new. And that's exciting because we don't know what that would look like. We get the opportunity to recreate a church that just might look more like the Jesus we are now studying, who has brown skin, and who hung out with all the bad folks.

This sense of embracing uncertainty is necessary for the whole work of reparation. Often when we, as white folk, think about reparations, we think about it as a means toward reconciliation, a finished product of racial harmony. But, as Fisher-Stewart taught me, we can't be racially "re-conciled" because we were never "conciled" to begin with.

We were never one. Black people and white people have never been one in the history of this nation. If we're trying to become one community together, there's no roadmap for that. We have to feel our way forward.

So we have to face these questions seriously. And it has to be something more than "we'll give you money, now shut up." Because ultimately that's what the money is. It's to shut us up. And we're saying, no. Money's nice, but, we're still not going to shut up.

We need something more. And it really takes being open and honest. And calling together people who would never voluntarily

*come to the table. In most of our anti-racist programs and Sacred
Ground, and other initiatives, people self-select for participation.
There are people who should be in these programs, but who have
no desire to be part of change, who like the church exactly the way
it is.*

That can seem very daunting, perhaps even a cause for
despair. If the process of repentance continues as far into the
future as we can imagine, if the steps forward are unknown and
uncertain, why even embark on the journey? The answer is that,
for all its hardship, the process of repentance and reparation is
fundamentally creative, imaginative, and hopeful. The process
itself provides the spiritual resources to sustain us on the path.

CHAPTER

7

Reparation

The allure of a blank slate is powerful. It's tempting to want to start from zero, and to say, "going forward, we will do rightly and justly," and so hope to put the past behind us. That will not serve. The past injuries of racism must be addressed, because they still impact the lives of Black and brown folk today. Imani shares her conversion on this point:

> *I used to be one of those negro Americans who, whenever reparations came up in conversation, would say, "That's not going to happen. That's a waste of your time. We should focus on things that are achievable."*
>
> *But the more I studied, the more I learned, the more I realized that reparations, in that basic sense of repairing harm that's been done, are profoundly necessary.*

There's an analogy that's often used to describe white privilege. The image is a sprint, a race between a Black runner and a white one. The Black runner has been dragged far behind the starting line, giving their white competitor a decisive lead before the race starts. On top of this, the Black competitor's path is strewn with obstacles: sand pits, water traps and hurdles, while their white opponent runs on a straight, flat track.

The image helps clarify the fact that white privilege is not merely some unmerited advantage bestowed on white people, but is, in fact, the corollary of unjust disadvantages imposed on Black and brown people. We are privileged precisely in the measure that people of color are oppressed.

It is true that God calls us toward an outlook of abundance, where we acknowledge the reality that there is enough for everyone to thrive. But we must also honestly recognize that the math of privilege and oppression is, in fact, a zero-sum equation. Racial equity requires whites to release unjustly amassed resources and advantages, so they can be used creatively to refill the voids of under-resourcing and disadvantage that undermine Black and brown communities, allowing everyone to operate on an equitable, and level field of play. This is reparations. As Imani puts it this way:

> When you look at the things people are demanding: jobs, land, education, housing, these are things everyone needs. These things are very basic human guarantees. When we look at these basic needs from our Western capitalist context, the idea is that we should all be eating off the plate, getting the same opportunities. But that's not how it works. I'm the one that's carrying these shaky plates, dealing with the heat of the coffee urn, and serving you. But I don't get to eat.
>
> Reparations is saying that this historical wrong, that happened, and is still going on, has got to begin to be made right, somewhere, sometime.

It so happens that this process is also central to Jesus's teaching on the Kingdom of God. The reversals of fortune that characterize Jesus's description of the Kingdom, where the first will be last and the last will be first, where the hungry are filled with good things and the rich are sent away empty, are often thought of as blessings for the afflicted and curses for the comfortable.

Certainly, Jesus uses this language in Luke's account of the Beatitudes.

But another way to think about it is that the humbling of the lofty and the exalting of the humbled are two sides of the same equation, necessary to bring both parties to equity and right relationship. Those who have been unjustly pressed down and those who have been unfairly raised up must walk different paths to come to the wide, level ground of the kingdom. One must be liberated, the other humbled. These are both graces.

The most dramatic showing of these reversals comes in the story of Zacchaeus. We meet a man who has raised himself high by aligning himself with a colonial power and enriching himself on the back of his neighbor's struggle. But he's physically short, so he finds himself humbled when a crowd gathers around Jesus. He can't see the teacher. So he exalts himself again, climbing high in a tree above the heads of his community. Jesus calls him down, humbling Zacchaeus again, and then invites himself over to Zacchaeus's house for lunch, exalting him one last time. The reversals come at a dizzying pace, and stop only when Zacchaeus makes a choice for reparation: a promise to return half his wealth to the poor, and pay back four times over whatever he has stolen. In response Jesus declares, "Today salvation has come to this house." Jesus only speaks this promise of salvation after Zacchaeus commits to repair. For whites, and or the institutions we control, reparations are a pre-condition for salvation.

Putting aside biblical interpretation and returning the analogy of the sprint, the image of the footrace reveals the difference between repentance and reparations. The structural changes repentance demands speak to dismantling institutional obstacles that sabotage the well-being and success of Black and brown folk. This is akin to removing the sand traps, water pits and hurdles that would hamstring the Black runner once the race has begun.

Reparations speak to remedying harms which occurred in the past but still continue to undermine communities of color, and advantage white communities today. This is akin to allowing the Black runner to leave the position where they've been held back, and advance to the starting line.

I admit, the analogy isn't perfect, but it helps clarify the difference between repentance and repair, and highlights why both are necessary. It is laudable, and important, for white institutions to remove structural obstacles to racial equity as they show up in hiring and leadership decisions, investment choices, admission policies and the like. Because these obstacles exist on a subconscious and cultural level within our institutions, it is also advisable to set specific targets of affirmative action to ensure more equitable outcomes. This can be a first step toward reparation. This is how Memorial Church began their work:

> As a church, we try to rest on theological understandings. We drew heavily from Isaiah 58, which concludes that we're called to be repairers of the breach and bind up things that are broken.
>
> There is this scriptural understanding that we as God's people have at various times in our history, broken covenant by God, by damaging each other, and the only way to come back into relationship with each other and God is to begin to seek repair and restitution. That became our theological grounding.

For Maggiano and Memorial, that theological grounding was important, when it came time to have tough conversations. They wrestled with the need to change leadership in the church to be more reflective of the city of Baltimore, which led to being intentional about how they select decision-makers, and how they recruit staff, and what kind music they choose, and who they choose to be on altar, and how they recruit ushers, making the outward face of the church more reflective of who they desire to be.

> *When I got there for my first Sunday, I looked around the altar, and without exception, everyone around me was a white man. There was diversity in terms of age and sexual orientation, but we were all white men.*
>
> *There were also symbols in our building that were doing harm. There were these plaques in the back. We had some folk working at the church who were asking themselves, "How can I work at this church when they're honoring people who enslaved my ancestors?" There was a huge triptych of the Transfiguration in the back with Jesus as a very, very, white man. We had work to do.*

Memorial, like many congregations, needed to tear down its own institutional barriers to equity. But, if these white institutions only remove racist obstacles within their own current structures, without addressing past harms, Black and brown folk will still be operating as a disadvantage because of the ongoing effects of those harms. In fact, if we only repent of current racist practices, without doing the concomitant work of reparation, we may find ourselves simply repeating old patterns of racist abuse. Maggiano reflected:

> *I think a similar dynamic is at play in the Episcopal Church. We see so many white men retire from bishop positions, often retiring early, to take more lucrative jobs. They're getting replaced by women and people of color who then have to do the hard work of being a bishop, that these white bishops did not want to do. They step away, but they'll still be in positions of authority over money and power within the church. So I wonder if we need to have a*

superstructure above bishops either formally or informally to con-
trol power and how it's shared.

Fisher-Stewart raises a similar concern, but with more pointed attention to the personal experience of the women of color who take these positions, and what "the hard work of being a bishop" looks like (for instance) to a Black woman who finds herself alone and in a position of leadership over a white institution.

> *We've seen this cohort of Black bishops elected. But I don't care what your race is, in the Episcopal Church, in the continental U.S., you're going to be a Black bishop of a white diocese. You may have sprinklings of color within the diocese, but it's going to be a white diocese. And so many of the bishops are getting called to exceptionally white dioceses. Sunday after Sunday you'll visit these congregations, and you may be the only person of color there. How does that make you feel? How does it feel to sit in your staff meetings and you are the only person of color? Why would you even go there? And why would they call you to serve?*
>
> *As we see this crop of Black bishops, we've got to start asking some questions. How many bishops of color have canons to the ordinary, or chiefs of staff, who are also of people of color? When you came in as Bishop, you could change all this. Why didn't you? These are questions we need to address.*

If we don't address these questions, if we don't deliver the resources and institutional support this new cohort of Black bishops deserve and need, then we must face the truth that we have, effectively, offered them up as sacrifices to assuage our collective white guilt.

Outside the realm of organization politics, we can consider how, on average, people of color won't have access to the same stores of parental wealth to fund parochial school educations, or studies at religious colleges. Their families were sabotaged from building that generational wealth. For the same reason, recent Black and brown graduates might find it difficult to accept the sort of lower paying entry positions churches often expect young clergy and lay religious professionals to start at. They are carrying more student loan debt, have fewer familial resources to fall back on, and may feel a greater responsibility to help support extended family networks that have also been sabotaged by white supremacy. When predominantly white institutions submit requests for proposals, Black and brown owned businesses, on average, will have lower capital resources, and more constrained professional networks, limiting their capacity to field competitive bids, even in an overtly equitable selection process. This again is a legacy of white supremacist harm. Ayers provides a detailed account of this legacy in the context Washington, DC:

> *Currently in DC, white people have eighty-one times the wealth of Black people, which is insane. The effect of that gap shows up in a thousand different ways.*
>
> *We live in a capitalist society: you have to have money to go to school. You have to have money to get quality health care. You have to have money to live in the right neighborhood, to send your kids to the right school.*

Ayers explains that when people are financially disadvantaged it affects everything. Her parents used to tell her they were trying to get her as close to the starting line as they could.

> *And I always wondered, "Wait, why am I behind?" I didn't get it. My dad grew up in rural Mississippi. My mom was more middle class, her father was a principal, but they weren't thriving.*

You could look around the corner, you would see families that had old money, crushing it out there. If we want to see people progress and grasp opportunities that are essential to the "American dream," they need money.

As we consider that gap, it's essential that we dispel from our thinking any illusions that this gap is a matter of happenstance or disaster. It has been engineered. The white community has enriched itself at the price of the Black community's impoverishment.

We know, as historical fact, that so many white people in this country are in the position they're in because of the free labor that was taken; because they stole Black people, and their ancestors stole Black people. Think about all that money.

Say Black people had been paid appropriately for their labor for all those years, and had saved it, and had the same opportunities as white people to invest. The wealth gap would not exist. We wouldn't be in a situation where most Black families don't have a dime to pass onto their children.

Ayers asserts that, if we're going to tackle reparations, we must address the racial wealth gap. This requires, once again, an unwillingness to accept easy answers. This requires us to squarely recognize the impoverishment of Black communities, without accepting it as just "an unfortunate reality." Where did the racial wealth gap come from? Why does it continue to widen? We need to develop a longing for honest accounting, and hunger for the truth of it. Ayers has that hunger.

We need to talk about why so many Black people are taking on reverse mortgages, especially older Black women here in the District. Why is that happening? I need answers.

More than just answers, we need to keep our hearts and minds focused on the human consequence of the answers we discover. Numbers tell a story. They ground that story in facts. But the meaning of that story is what matters. What does the wealth gap mean for the daily lives of people who've been shoved into it?

Black people have been significantly financially disadvantaged in this country. That impacts our health care, our mental health, our education, and even our political agency. You see all these politicians, and these political action committees that have some much money at their disposal, And when you start digging into it, you discover it's old money that's backing them.

Alongside the injuries and deprivations caused by this impoverishment, there is also the hurt of lost possibility: the pain of wondering what could have been.

If we had that same kind of backing here in the District, what would our city look like? What would our political influence look like? Or what would our impact on the nation at large look like if we didn't have a racial wealth gap? Reparations has to include something that makes a concerted effort to close that gap.

Complementing Ayers's pragmatic framing regarding the need for reparations, Knapper offers a moral frame for understanding the need to make reparation for harms of the past, and a vision for the creative possibilities we can encounter if we undertake it.

I think that Mutual Aid is definitely centered on the idea that there is a very serious resource gap. And it's not just a gap, but an institutionalized structure. Old institutions in this country were built on the idea of plundering resources and withholding from vulnerable communities. Those communities aren't naturally vulnerable, these institutions we're talking about create those vulnerabilities. That is fundamentally how these institutions were able to amass the power they have.

A lot of people use the language of broken systems. I reject that, because I think that our institutions aren't broken, they're functioning in the way that they were intended to.

One response in the face of systems that were designed to plunder and sabotage, is to opt out, and create alternative structures that are designed differently, designed to promote health.

Because of the way that imbalance of power exists, there should be an emphasis on building power amongst folks who have been left out of decision-making spaces, who've been left out of access to resources, who've been left out of the position of even being able to create a level playing field, who have not been able to fully thrive because of the oppression that they have experienced as a result of these institutions and these systems

The fact of the matter is, none of these spaces are going to decide on their own to give up that power, or to hand the resources they have stolen back to the folks they've stolen them from. They're not going to do that on their own.

For this reason (among others) many organizers striving for the liberation and uplift of Black and brown communities choose to spend their time and efforts supporting Black and brown communities directly, rather than lobbying predominantly white institutions that sabotage them.

These communities have the agency to create resources on their own, within their own neighborhoods, within their own communities.

They're creating their own systems of care in order to fill these very large gaps that exist now because of these long-term institutional biases.

But, Knapper acknowledges, there are limits to what we can accomplish by being the change we want to see. It is good to light a lamp rather than curse the dark. But, if your lamp oil has been stolen, you need to get it back, if you hope to find your way home.

It's unrealistic, not even just unrealistic, but dangerous, to believe that it stops with creating the resources that we need ourselves within these spaces, without acknowledging that we are owed so much from the people that took so much from us. Accountability has to be part of these infrastructures of care that we are creating.

I don't think that a vulnerable community should put all of its energy into accountability processes. But I do think that we live in a country, we live in a city, that is so rich, literally, financially, resource rich, that there has to be a reckoning for returning that wealth to the people that built this country, and that's really what reparations is for me.

To put it another way, if we remove all obstacles from the track, leaving Black competitors to do their own thing unimpeded, but still require them to start the race thirty yards behind white runners, it can hardly be called fair. Ayers describes wrestling with both sides of this equation in her work:

At DC Justice Lab we're trying to work holistically on everything we can accomplish, across the entire spectrum of harms. For criminal justice reform, we have three buckets we're working on: policing, prosecution and punishment. We start at the beginning: trying to limit interactions between police and Black people because they keep ending up deadly. If we shift that dynamic, we limit the ongoing harm.

Working down the spectrum, you eventually get to punishment. Now we're talking about people getting imprisoned and going to jail. At that point, the harm's been done. And reparation is necessary. Both the bills I'm working on speak to that harm or post-harm phase. So they're both reparations in some sense.

Expungement and record sealing is a step on the way to reparations. We are trying to stop punishing people first: that's the harm. But how do you repair harms for people who've already been punished, who were impacted, for instance, by the war on drugs, people who still have marijuana convictions on their record, despite the fact that it's been decriminalized here in DC? Now they have criminal records that they're saddled with for years and decades. They're not able to get jobs they want, or the security clearance that they need to move up and get a promotion, or to live where they want to live, or volunteer at their kid's school, or be the kind of parent that they want to be. And they have no relief.

They're holding onto the trauma of this mistake they made, or of being wrongfully accused. And they aren't allowed to move on. They did their time. Enough is enough. But they're still stigmatized as criminals. And that baggage is really harmful. The first step is to get it off their records.

Repentance alone is insufficient. Reparation is required. On the other hand, if white institutions work to make reparations for the harms of the past, without going through repentance and the structural reform it requires, they will continue to perpetuate the harms that required reparation in the first place: offering band-aids for wounds of the past with one hand, while inflicting new wounds with the other. Reparations alone are insufficient. Repentance is required. Ayers lays out the relationship between them:

I can sit here and craft a perfect plan for reparations. Let's say, off the top of my head, we every descendant of slave in Washington, DC, a hundred thousand dollars. That would be a great cash transfer. And boom, you could say, "We got it done." You close the racial wealth gap. But if you still have a criminal record, and you cannot get a job, and you cannot do the things that you need to do because you're being held back, how long will it be before that gap re-emerges? How much has really been repaired if I'm still getting pulled over by the police all the time?

I think the way reparations and structural change tie together is that it's a massive quilt of, of reducing harm, and creating a safe and free DC. We're going to push for whatever parts of it we can get through. But in an ideal world, they're all interconnected, they all work together.

To get all the parts working together smoothly (or at a minimum, to avoid throwing a wrench into the works), white institutions need to be able to distinguish clearly between repairing the racist harms of the past, and repenting from future racist harm. If not, they will fall short in understanding the fullness of what's required on both sides. We will tend to reckon our efforts of repentance as counting toward reparation and our efforts at reparation as counting toward repentance. They don't.

A number of white institutions have undertaken equity initiatives that they label reparations. There includes such policies as "set-asides," designating that a certain portion of service contracts be granted to Black and brown owned companies, or setting particular hiring targets for diversity, or establishing priority enrollment for the Black and brown students, or creating endowments to fund positions that will be staffed by people of color.

These are good policies that predominantly white institutions should take on. But they are not reparation. First, because they address current inequitable practices. In essence, these policies try to get our institutions to do what they should have been doing from the start: granting equitable opportunity and access to the institution's resources.

But second, most of these policies still operate under a transactional model. Set-aside contracts, or priority hiring, or endowed staff positions are still fee-for-service arrangements: the white institution is receiving something material in exchange for the resources it offers. We can be grateful if the transaction is equitably, it should, but this can't, by definition, be considered recompense for past harm.

Reparations, in some sense, are payment on a debt. Therefore, by definition, white individuals and institutions should receive nothing in exchange for the reparations they make, or else it is not reparations. Reparations necessarily entail an aspect of release and surrender.

This also means that white institutions must let go of the purse strings. Many white institutions have undertaken reparations initiatives by establishing "impact grant" funds, which these same institutions administer, or, at minimum, maintain significant oversight for. This easily, and often, moves into the realm of white institutions making decisions about what constitutes "worthy" use of reparations funds. This is not reparations. It is charity. And it is patronizing. Imani offers a kind of internal check that can be helpful in distinguishing whether the work we are discussing is genuinely reparations, or if it is just charity:

> *The difference is a stiff resolve to create space where people can think clearly enough to articulate their larger problems for themselves.*

If I'm risking my life, and my family's life, to panhandle on the side of the road, just to get by, there are systemic reasons I can't have a conversation with you about the same systemic reasons that keep me there. I can't unpack those things because I'm physically hungry. I don't have space to think about it. My brain won't work in that setting.

But if you share something to eat, let me get my bearings, let me catch my breath, help make sure my family is safe at the moment, now, while we're eating, I've got bandwidth to tell you how this started. I can tell you my husband had a workman's comp claim that was denied. Our insurance wouldn't cover it. Medical bills bankrupted us, and we lost our house.

And then you ask, "Well, didn't you have any savings?" And I can say, "No, I didn't, because we're low wage migrant workers." And then you can ask, "Well, what about your parents, couldn't they help?" And I can say, "No, I was separated from them." There are policy decisions all along the way that shape that story.

Charity is good. Because people need to eat. But if we're talking about repair, we need to leverage charity to make room so people who are directly affected by these challenges can define their own problems and determine how best to solve them. Is your charity helping people do that?

One question that comes up repeatedly in these discussions is: "What's the difference between charity and reparations?" There are many layers, and many answers to this question, but it's hard to miss this central refrain: "it's a question of who makes the choices." If the community that has been harmed is not at the table making decisions about how resources will be offered, you are certainly doing charity. But if that same directly impacted community is engaged, shaping the process and guiding outcomes, it is more likely that you're taking on reparation. It is not for white individuals or institutions to decide what is best for Black and brown communities. It is for us to make good on a debt owed for four hundred years of abuse. Imani continues:

> *A lot of organizations around the country talking about repara-tions have set these targets, where they're going to give away such and such amount of money. And they're going to do it through these grants. Fine, great.*
>
> *But you're still deciding who gets what. You're still putting yourself in the position of power. You're deciding who's worthy. And you're making these marginalized people, people you've done harm to, jump through these hoops, and do this song and dance to receive repair. Why should the people you've exploited have to exploit themselves even more, to get what's owed? It comes down to dignity. Do the people that you are claiming to help have dig-nity in your process?*

As you begin building your processes and structures for making and offering reparation, creating "space where people can think clearly enough to articulate their larger problems for themselves," is essential. Respecting and protecting the dignity and agency of directly-impacted community representatives who graciously offer their leadership, is essentially. It must be written, explicitly, into words of policy for your organization, that everyone can see, and refer back to. But explicit policy, alone will be insufficient. We must fundamentally shift our perspective to leave charity behind and step toward reparation. Imani offered this invocation:

> *It's about more than just one example or one problem. We have to change our mindset. We've been raised in colonialism so long, we don't even know how not to be colonial anymore. We've lived with this thing so long, we actually think it's good.*

At its worst, this tendency to be bound by our colonial imagination, even when we approach a task like reparations, can have down-right cringey results. Imani recalled:

> *I was on a call recently. There were these organizations that are looking to hire Black people to do some random Black stuff for some other random Black people, just so they can feel like they're doing something about diversity. And it's patronizing. It's like "Here's some watermelons. Black people like that."*

Her comment brought up the memory of recently attending a county-wide Juneteenth celebration, with my family. Apart from myself, the only other white people I saw were a group of vendors, selling watermelons. They seemed to think they were contributing to the celebration, and looked perplexed at the festival goers passing by, all of whom cut a wide circle to keep distance, as if their stall was surrounded by an invisible wall. This is what happens when white people make choices unilaterally about what Black people need. It's not a good look.

The Black communities around this country are those best qualified to identify what they need, and how that debt for four hundred years of sabotage and theft should be paid. Baxter describes how the Task Force on Black Ministries for the EDOW has identified, named and shared the specific needs of Black congregations, by taking the time to listen to their own stakeholders.

> *There's a couple simple things we've found are important to help Black congregations. The first is connecting with the community around you. That's very important. You've got to understand what's going on in your neighborhood: the dynamics of what's changing, what's new, what community assets and resources are in the area.*

Another crucial element is leadership development within the congregation. You can't have a cookie cutter solution for the issues facing Black churches though, because so much depends on the different circumstances of each congregation and their surroundings. So we need the flexibility and the leadership capacity to be able to adapt. That leadership is something we need to build, not just among clergy, but among laity as well. Often that responsibility gets laid at the feet of the ordained ministers. But we need to get laity on board if we're going to accomplish the kind of shifts in thinking we need. So we've discovered the need to design programs and training specifically for leadership within the church.

To offer an example from a predominantly white institution, Memorial Church, under Maggiano's leadership, give a practical picture of what it looks like to follow the decisions and leadership of the community to whom reparations are owed:

You have to be attentive to the power dynamics of who controls the power, where the money goes, and who controls where the money goes. When we first got started we put together a reparations group, and one of the initial ideas was to take all the reparations money and put it in a separate bank account, at a Black-owned bank, and give it over to a group of Black community members to choose what to do with it. And it seemed like a great idea to us.

But we had this Reparations Committee made up of community members. And they said, "If you give us responsibility for spending all the money and we don't do it the way you want to, you're going to blame us, and this is going to end. If you give folks responsibility without giving authority, or give responsibility without giving power, you're just shuffling off the work you don't want to do onto somebody else."

We heard back from this Black-owned bank that the amount of money we were talking about wasn't enough to impact the bank's position. And that they weren't set up, or designed to handle the kind of transactions we were talking about. So they said, it doesn't help us, and you guys are going to get frustrated. You're going to blame the bank. Then it's going to hurt the bank's reputation. So it's going to be more of a hassle than it's a benefit for anybody. Those were really important lessons about power and responsibility.

Living into these lessons of power and responsibility will require our churches to radically shift how we engage in outreach. Churches like to be in charge and call the shots. We like to be seen as leaders in the community. We like to be recognized for our good deeds. If memory serves, Jesus has some things to say about these tendencies. Maggiano talks about the reorientation his church went through as they undertook the process of reparations.

We often will do things performatively in the church, while still retaining hold of the actual power. So instead we have to do the reverse, where we put the onus on the church and the church staff and administration to, to allocate the money, to spend the money, to deliver the money. But the authority for where it goes is entirely on the reparations committee. And we don't ask anything in return, there's no oversight entity reporting on it, there's no accounting demanded. You don't have to provide statistics to justify some grant. It's reparations.

That attention to power and who has it is essential because what needs to be repaired is the relationship between people. An important part of the work is restoring and healing relationships between communities, between churches, between Black churches and white churches. White churches in Black neighborhoods and

*Black churches in white neighborhoods. There has to be a real con-
nection and relationship that's developed.*

Following this example, we should strive to create structures of reparation that maximize the authority of the community that has been harmed in deciding how resources will be
used and dispersed, while maximizing the responsibility of the
white institution for carrying out those decisions.

Imani lifts up another point of distinction between charity
and reparations. Charity tends toward offering chronic, pallia-
tive care. Reparation works for transformation:

> *I heard a friend of mine talking about this idea of good medi-
> cine. He said good medicine is medicine that deals with a par-
> ticular problem, and then passes out of the body. It doesn't stick
> around.*
>
> *A lot of what those of us in this nonprofit industrial complex
> do is done in a very colonial way, where the help is designed to
> stick around forever. Those aren't the medicines we need.*

The final point of distinction Imani raises concerns the
question of motivation. Our intention as we engage the process will often be the deciding factor between whether we end
doing charity, or taking part in reparation:

> *It's always good to ask, "Why am I doing this?"*
>
> *If you're doing "good works" based out of white guilt, then
> you're going to center the need of your whiteness. You heard about
> some systemic problem, and it makes you feel bad. That feeling is
> what drives you. Therefore the solutions you come up with will
> serve the need of making you feel less bad.*
>
> *But feeling bad isn't the problem for me. I don't feel bad about
> these evil systems. I live in these systems. The systems themselves,
> not your feelings about them, are the problem for me. That's what*

drives me. Therefore the solutions I come up with will serve the need of dismantling these systems.

If you're really looking to repair a harm, and you ask some-one who's been directly impacted about it, they might bring out a facet of the problem you haven't considered. It might end up being the most important facet of the problem to address. So the question becomes: are you hearing from people who are impacted? Are you putting them in a position to be successful articulating their perspective to you? Are you addressing the systemic chal-lenges that might affect them? Are you addressing the systemic challenges that affect their ability to articulate their situation? Or are you staying on the cute level?

And then you have to push further, and ask yourself, are the solutions we're developing together lasting solutions that can automate at scale? Or are they fixes that will only benefit one or two members of the impacted group? We have enough mouth pieces. We have too many. We need to set up silent structures that move toward repair, and that don't depend on the energy or per-sonality of any one person.

There is no blueprint for these structures of authority, responsibility and accountability. They must be negotiated with the very people who have been harmed. I can say, from the first-hand experience of EDOW's Task Force, this process of negotiation can be deeply uncomfortable.

We will be tempted along the way to evade this discom-fort. One way that may show up is by distancing ourselves from the harms we seek to repair. In some sense, it is easier to address the racist harms our institutions have inflicted outside of themselves, rather than acknowledging and seeking to repair the racist harms that have been inflicted internally. There is a greater personal sense of conviction when we must face how we wronged our own colleagues and companions. It may be wise to begin with the place of greatest discomfort. Baxter shares the importance of this perspective when he describes the work of the Task Force on Black Ministries in this diocese:

In the current atmosphere, people worship where they feel comfortable. But we do know that there's a history in the Diocese of Washington, as churches began to become more Black, or when more Black people were moving to a certain area, some members of these churches split and moved part of the congregation to a new location.

This is a classic example of a social dynamic that we might be *inclined* to dismiss as "natural," "inevitable," or "harmless." After all, this is a question of people simply deciding to land where they feel comfortable. And many of us feel more comfortable in the company of those we identify as being "like us." There is no explicitly codified policy of segregation. It's a question of free choice. But this analysis belies the fact that our ideas of comfort, and our perceptions of "likeness" are conditioned by the racist assumptions of our society. More importantly, this analysis ignores how the "free choice" of white members to leave a community as it becomes increasingly Black, has racialized consequences for how resources are distributed.

It put those institutions that they left behind at a disadvantage monetarily, as well as in a whole host of other things. And we know that's not unique to the history of Washington, DC. Throughout most of the throughout the United States there's history where certain congregations have received more resources and assets, both in terms of their creation, and in terms of their later support. That's been an issue within our Black churches. They weren't given the resources that other congregations received, resources they need to thrive and be viable today.

There are reams and reams of paper published on the topic of church revitalization. You could paper the walls of a cathedral with all strategic plans for congregation growth circulating in mainline denominations now. Fewer have been published with the specific needs and concerns of Black congregations in mind. Fewer still have been drafted by Black leaders for Black congregations within mainline denominations. And still fewer yet have been resourced adequately to have a chance at success. Baxter lays it out plainly:

> *It's nice to have all these ideas, but you have to fund them. Churches want to expand their music ministries to enhance their worship services. But if you don't have money, you can't get the musicians you need. Some type of dedicated funding is critically important. That's tied to the reparations work. If we really want to see our church become viable and thriving you need a dedicated funding source to equip leaders within those organizations to be able to try new things, and know they can tinker with program changes that get them vibrant and growing.*

For me, Baxter's use of the word "tinker" is telling. Predominantly white churches, and other predominantly white institutions, often have the financial wherewithal to engage in the process of learning by trial and failure. They can afford to experiment. Which will eventually lead successful strategies for growth. Black and brown churches often won't have the financial reserves, or the social capital or credit within the institution to risk trying new strategies that might not be successful at first go. This inequality must be redressed. For those of us who are white ministers, this requires acknowledging that our Black and brown colleagues have been working with their hands tied by the need to be immediately successful on the first attempt, whereas we have been allowed the freedom to tinker. That is a convicting and uncomfortable realization. But it is one that we must face if we hope to come to equity.

Acknowledging the importance of internal reparations work, we must also recognize that both internal and external reparations are necessary. In fact, they are deeply interdependent. Baxter lays out this connection:

> There's a clear link between them. As to what a structure of repair that connects both might look like, that will require a robust discussion. But I see them as clearly linked.
>
> In my opinion, you can't very well have a discussion about reparations for the wider community, without also doing internal examination as to what damage may have been done in your own house and your own institution, specifically with regard to Black churches.
>
> You have to do that hard, introspective work. You're going to have to ask, where have you contributed to this damage in society? Where have we done that in our own house? Did we decide that this one church would get more resources and support than that one over there? And why did we decide that?
>
> So yes, they're linked. You've got to have the conversation about reparations owed to the larger Black community. But it's got to start at home first.

This tension between the need to repair institutional racist harms inflicted both within and without the institution is only one of the tensions we must navigate as we consider making reparations. We must be committed for the long term, and be prepared to keep focus even as many other very legitimate needs and crises land before us, demanding attention and priority for our resources. As Knapper notes, negotiating between the long-term vision of reparation, and the urgent needs that come knocking is not easy. But it is essential:

> *There is no perfect answer to this. I've been talking with a lot of people about this recently. There is a responsibility to meet as much of the urgent need as we can, whether we're talking about the Supreme Court, or whether we're talking about the migrants being bused into DC, or the very real housing crisis this city is facing and has been facing for a long time, or the public health crisis around COVID, or now, Monkeypox, and this list goes on and on. There are always going to be crises that need to be met in the moment.*
>
> *We also need to understand that most of these crises are created, either intentionally, or through the lack of response from larger systems that are intentionally designed to work this way.*
>
> *As long as all of us here on the ground, who care about this work and care about each other, and who are impacted by this, are in a state of constant emergency we are distracted from dealing with the system that has forced us to be in this state of crisis. And because of that, we will not have the time or capacity to deal with the roots of these problems.*
>
> *We have to do what we can to meet some of the immediate needs. But one thing that I tell vulnerable communities that I'm in relationship with is "We did not create these circumstances."*
>
> *So it is not for us to hold all the energy and work of fixing a thing that we did not cause. The more time we spend all of our energy doing exactly that, the more we are helping these systems continue to operate in these harmful ways.*

A third tension in this work is inherent in the very act of making reparations at all. Reparations aim to address harms racist harms caused by our institutions. In some sense, they are necessarily backward-looking. But, in their application and use, reparations look forward, toward possibilities beyond our current systems of oppression. That forward-looking work is the heart of Knapper's organizing.

> *I choose to spend most of my organizing energy thinking about what kind of systems we can create separate from existing systems of harm. How can we create care and resources for each other? One of the major issues of concern for us, in the mutual aid networks, is creating food; creating systems of urban farming so we can make our own food. How are we creating cooperative spaces for housing? How can we build housing co-ops and food co-ops? How can we build alternative systems to fill our needs?*
>
> *While we're working to move those other big systems toward reparations and accountability, and waiting for that to happen, we need to ask, "how are we keeping each other safe right now?" Practically and concretely, right now, and that is about building something outside of these systems. That's where my focus comes in.*

If reparations is not about creation, it's not reparations. If it's not about partnering with sabotaged communities and those made vulnerable in building their own well-being, safety, and opportunity, then it isn't reparations at all. In this sense, the attention of reparations is always toward health, not illness, justice, not inequity, and liberation, not white supremacy. But reparations themselves arise from within a sick, inequitable, and white supremacist system, and must be attentive to those realities. Knapper often operates in that fraught quagmire:

> *A good portion of my work is definitely working within a very rotten system. So I think accountability s important.*

Reparations, as practice, must aim to hold predominantly white and white dominated institutions accountable for systems and a history a racist abuse. But, if our practice of reparations fails to point beyond those systems and history, then there is a real danger we are only dragging out and feeding attention to those systems. If reparations offer only visible criticism/accountability, without achieving substantive change, then there is a real danger our efforts at reparations will be co-opted as propaganda to provide cover for the very systems of harm we hope to confront. And so, Knapper advises us:

> *Accountability cannot be the center of the work that we are doing, because if we are not truly investing in breaking the cycles of harm, breaking the cycles, not just trying to work within them, if we are not invested in that, we're going to be living in crisis forever, we're going to be living in a state of emergency forever. I'm pretty exhausted with living that way.*

C. S. Lewis quips: "There are two equal and opposite errors into which our race can fall about the devils. One is to disbelieve in their existence. The other is to believe, and to feel an excessive and unhealthy interest in them." This summarizes the tension we must hold in our attention to white supremacy as we undertake reparations. We must understand, and remain constantly aware of the structures of white supremacy which we aim to dismantle, without letting those structures eclipse our attention the alternatives we hope to partner in building. For Knapper, the best way to check this balance is to assess the state of our collaborations:

> *It's about asking: "How am I creating alternatives? How am I building power with folks who have left out of the system?" It's not even right to say, "left out of the system," because we've been part of the system, but only in the sense of abusing our labor and then being tossed aside.*

So, whereas churches and other institutions generally like to get credit for starting something entirely new, the most effective and appropriate destination for reparations may be in supporting the kind of creative alternatives Knapper describes. In many cases, we may learn the communities to whom we owe reparations have been working to build these alternatives for years. Our reparations then, might work to resource the work they've already been doing. Knapper's focus toward creating alternative sustainable structures for community support speaks to an essential aspect of reparations: mending the harms, both structural, and culturally colonial, that have sabotaged the autonomy of Black and brown communities. For those of us who hang our hopes on a vision of racial reconciliation, this may seem oxymoronic, because it means accepting that reparations is partly about creating circumstances where integration is not necessary, or expected. Fisher-Stewart hold up one example of what this looks like:

> I look at the Indigenous Anglicans in Canada. They've said: "Well, let us offer you this. Let us fix the church. They want an Indigenous church. A couple of weeks ago, they started a call process for an Indigenous Bishop. They do have Indigenous bishops in the Anglican church, but they want an Indigenous Bishop for the Indigenous church because, they say, this is the only way we are going to be able to incorporate our customs, our traditions, our faith beliefs, into the church. You all want to do the Anglican thing every Sunday, and then put our culture on display, once or twice a year, like we do here in the US with Black Episcopalians. But they're saying, we want a church that acknowledges that our belief system is just as valid as the dominant belief system. They want their own readings of scripture to be accepted as just as normative and valid.

They've given themselves permission—the various nations, and various tribes to develop their own prayers, their own liturgies. And the Indigenous Anglicans are saying no, we don't just want window dressing. If you will change your governance system, if you will change your liturgies, if you will change your belief systems, if you will add to them ours, then perhaps we can be part of you, but you're not going to do that. Therefore, we must separate ourselves. We will still be Anglicans. We will still be part of an Anglican Communion, but it would be the Indigenous church.

Now you could say Black people did that here. We had the Black church, for that very same reason. Unfortunately, in this country, the drive, the need to assimilate, is too great. So the Black church has lost a lot of the traditions that were brought over from Africa to include how we saw and dealt with Christianity. We're at the point where you have Black folks who turn up their noses when you say we need libations to start the service, or include the ring shout. People will say no, we can't do that. And that attitude is a harm, caused by the white church.

Just as truly embracing the work of reparations might require us to defer, or relinquish our hopes of racial reconciliation, it may also require us to accept the impossibility of the task. Fisher-Stewart returns to the example of Indigenous Anglicans in Canada:

Over a few years they've gotten twenty or twenty-five million dollars from the church and the government, to repair the damage done by residential schools.

For them, it's in the past, but also present. They can actually put their finger on the harm. They can say: "Let's look at residential schools, and the abuses there." They can also say: "Let's look at the theft of Indigenous lands, because probably every church is sitting on somebody else's land." It's specific. And you can look for specific responses: improving education and healthcare and mid-wifery and all of these things.

But ultimately, the Indigenous Anglicans have said: "You can do all that, but guess what? It'll never make up for the damage that has been done. You can give us more money and more money, but it will never deal with the trauma inflicted, historically, generationally and intergenerationally. And it won't fix what currently ails us."

It's deeply humbling, convicting, and painful to acknowledge that the harms our institutions have participated in may cut so deep they can never truly be healed. It threatens to throw all our utopian hopes of "racial reconciliation" out the window and calls the whole endeavor of reparations into question. But it does no one any good to ignore this possibility. It's a truth we must face. Ayers says:

When you're sitting in grief with people, and you're feeling it internally, which I do, being a descendant of slaves on both sides, you have to face the fact that you cannot make up for four hundred years of trauma. Even if we're really trying to repair that long history of how Black people have been treated, or Native American people have been treated in the US, you can't get those years back. You cannot make up for what my parents experienced when their schools were integrated. You have to be sober minded about that and honest.

At the same time, the recognition of this fact cannot be taken as an excuse not to try. Full repair may rest beyond our reach, but we are obliged to pursue it, nonetheless. We must make the attempt.

We've got to try our best to rectify tangible and real harms, in the places we can make a measurable impact to benefit folks.

That's my argument, when people say, "It's been so long," or "It's too much," or "It's too big." I say, "Something is better than nothing, right?" It may be a band-aid, compared to what it should have looked like if we'd done this right in 1865, when slavery was being wrapped up. Or what it could have looked like in the Jim Crow era. But making an effort to do something is exponentially better than sitting on it and saying we're going to do nothing. Even if it doesn't measure up to the full scale of the harm, it would mean the United States acknowledging: "We messed up. We did this wrong. This was evil. This was wrong. We're not going to sugarcoat this. We're not going to try to make this sound better than it was. We were wrong. And this is what we can do to start making it right."

Not only must we make the attempt at reparations, despite the insufficiency, but we must strive to do better than our first attempt, or our second or our third. As Fisher-Stewart notes, it may never be enough. But there is always the possibility of doing better. As anyone who's taken a long trip knows, you'll never reach the horizon, but that doesn't mean you aren't moving forward. Ayers offers this powerful exhortation:

We must push that as far as we can go. We don't settle and say, "Hey, this is the best we could do." The best we can do, is not the best we can do. We should push, and push, and push. And if it takes us four different tries and rounds of policy to get it right, then let's keep pushing. Let's keep doing that deep listening. Let's keep doing better. Let's keep finding new places to rectify this.

As you can see by now, the pictures of what reparations might look like are diverse, wide and surprising. In the push to "do something" there are temptation and danger to prematurely close the conversation and our own imagination, to settle on a single course of action we can follow. Nearly all the partners I've spoken with have warned against this. Imani poignantly frames the dangers of narrowing our vision too early, alongside the possibilities of what could be, if we take the time to open ourselves to God's grander visions:

> *We take the way things are as the way they've always been, and the way they'll always be. And that limits our imagination. When we're talking about repair, we're talking about building something that we haven't seen yet. We have to decolonize our thinking so we can imagine something new.*
>
> *We see that in the Bible, with the children of Israel. They've escaped slavery, but they're still stuck in the colonial thinking of Egypt. God and Moses are telling them: "You can be bold. You can do something different, do something just." But they struggle to hear it. We do too.*

When we consider the harms are realities of white supremacy, we're talking about a system that has endured and shaped the world for five centuries. We are, all of us, some fifteen or more generations removed from the last people who remember the world before its dominion took hold. We have no reference point to imagine alternatives beyond it. We might feel like a fish that someone has suddenly asked, "What does land looks like?"

But that's underestimating ourselves. And letting ourselves off the hook too easily. Five hundred years is a long time. But it's only a sliver in the grand story of humankind. We lived without white supremacy for a much longer time. We could find our way there again, but it will take deep self-interrogation, determined imagination and hard work. We may need to ask new questions entirely. Imani shares her personal growth around one particular corner of these racist harms: the criminal justice system:

I was one of those who, when people were talking about prison and police abolition, would ask, "But who's going to get the rapists and the murderers?" It takes a while to really ask the question with genuine curiosity: "How do we make sure people are safe?" And when you ask the question that way you notice: "Oh, wait, we can do something else?"

There are so many philosophical underpinnings we take for granted, and we need to question them if we're going to come with effective solutions. You have to dig in and interrogate yourself beyond the surface level.

This openness to new possibilities does not diminish the need to articulate a clear and robust vision of reparations. You'll need that vision to support and carry you along the path. I tell anyone who will listen that I think predominantly white churches should surrender 15% of total assets, including real estate, to Black-led organizations working for the economic empowerment and liberation of the Black community in their region. That is a clear and specific vision, and it sustains me.

But we must hold these visions lightly enough that we are prepared to revise them, or even abandon them and start over, in conversation and relationship with directly impacted stake-holders, that is, the communities to whom reparations are owed. Schulken typifies what it looks like to hold a clear and robust vision while holding it lightly.

I want to see us complete what we are actively working on now. I want to see our diocese follow the example of the Diocese of Maryland and commit to providing the dollars and commit to working with Black organizations in the community to make reparations, not the reparations that we think ought to be made, but working with them to help achieve what they decide is the best way forward.

I want to be sure we're not just writing a check and walking away. This work shouldn't be a one-and-done. It needs to continue at the diocesan level.

Schulken wants to see neighborhood and parish churches take the question seriously and start thinking about what needs to happen at the local level in to repair the breach. She recognizes that there's no shortcut to that. It is hard work that is never done.

Working at Grace with Kevin, the Black member in our parish history group, has been really interesting. At our last meeting he said, "even as we're discovering these really hard truths, we need to also look for the drops of goodness. Even when we're considering the horrors of enslaving another person, we have to see the humanity and complexity of the situation." I'm not sure what I think about that, but that phrase he used—"drops of goodness"— it's working around my brain and percolating in the back of my mind.

One growing edge for me, where I've been working to hold my vision very lightly, regards the place of financial assets in reparations. Fisher-Stewart recently challenged me to think more broadly about the question of reparations, and what it requires. I still believe financial redress is essential. Because there has been real theft, from the plunder of Indigenous lands, to enslavement, to the under-resourcing of Black congregations. There was wealth piled up through the plunder and I think there has to be a reckoning. But as Fisher-Stewart noted:

I hear you. But I really wonder if they're serious about doing that. If they are serious then for me, I don't need a check, I really don't.

But let's say we're going to go over to Southeast DC and we're going to build up this school that's been under-resourced. We're going to make sure that Black kids who want to go to the Episcopal schools have the opportunity for that. But we're also doing something in the community. We are going to pick two public schools in Southeast, and we are going to give them what they need. If we have to pay teachers, add onto their salaries so they can have a living wage and feel valued, then that's what we're going to do.

That way those families in wards seven and eight don't have to bus their kids someplace else in order to get a good education. They can do what the white folks do in ward three, send their kids to the school in their neighborhood.

There are ways. God provided enough for everybody. It's just that it all got hoarded. And if some of your people would just get off of it, folks would have what folks need to thrive. Everybody won't be driving a Maserati, but you'll be able to eat and get a decent education so you can take care of yourself.

There are things churches could do, if they wanted to. You want to help somebody, you could get a couple churches together and say we're going to pay off student loans for Black graduates coming out of college. And if you did that, your churches would be full. Your churches would be full with young Black people. But do they really want that?

While acknowledging the importance of financial redress, Fisher-Stewart challenged me to reorient, and consider that the central aim of reparations must and should be the establishment of right and just relationships across lines of race. Financial reparations are a necessary means to this end, but they are not an end unto themselves. If we fail to press onward to the goal of right relationship, we can expect whatever gains we achieve to be snatched away:

I still have hope that the Episcopal Church will do what it's called to do beyond the walls. To get out of the buildings and make a difference in people's lives. And so I look at this whole reparations thing as: yes, we need to repair the relationship. And we haven't been working on that in a substantive way.

It's been great to have a Black Presiding Bishop but he hasn't made a whole lot of change. No one person can do what needs to be done. Great preaching, great ideas. But we haven't seen transformation. And, when Bishop Curry leaves, I hope there's not that Obama backlash. But the reality is, this church is white because it wasn't to be white.

Just like this country after Obama, there are people who want their church back. They want somebody who doesn't channel his Baptist grandmother, who knows how to stay in the pulpit, and stays out of politics, who won't embarrass us in front of Her Majesty. And it gives that sense that we're not ready to have that conversation.

Bridging that gap, between our unreadiness to talk honestly and the urgent need to speak the truth, between the limits of our colonized imagination and the wide possibilities of God's grace is no simple feat. It may even seem impossible. We've all sat in on brainstorming sessions that go nowhere. We've all been there when some brave soul calls the central question, only to be met with silence.

This is another place where centering the leadership of directly impacted communities is crucial. I'm cautious about appealing to ideas of redemptive suffering. But it's hard not to notice the capacity for creative vision and lateral thinking communities afflicted by racist sabotage have developed. The pressure of surviving a white supremacist system has required these communities to develop methods for seeing, visioning, and imagining, what it takes to make a way where there is no way. These are precisely the skills needed to make plans for reparation. To take one example, Fisher-Stewart has collaborated extensively with Lorretta Woodward Veney, a public speaker who's used LEGO for everything from helping individuals process trauma, to guiding religious institutions in strategic plans, to supporting neighborhoods as they brainstorm solutions for gun violence.

> *It's almost magical this thing she does with LEGO bricks. You're in your own little world and you're building whatever it is that you're supposed to be building, and then you have to explain it and you go like, oh crap. And somehow you find a way to explain it.*
>
> *So maybe you could gather congregations and give them a task that uses art and ask, what is your understanding of the harm that was done? And you'd create a space for people to express it in some way, where they don't have to verbalize it; they use the art. But then they need to explain it once it's finished. That could help us get past the crickets, could help us list out the harms. And again, maybe we can't fix that. But at least it would be known.*

Given Fisher-Stewart's framing, that there needs to be a full reckoning, but that once the scope of the harm is known we may come to see that full restitution is impossible because the breadth and depth of the injury is too great, I asked if that implied, in some sense, that reparations are a fool's errand.

> *No. Because we may determine we can heal to a degree. Sometimes you get sick, you can only be healed to a degree. And you accept healing to that degree. And hoping that you stay in remission for a long while. And we just won't say, well, no, since we can't be healed completely, since we can't fix it completely, we are not going to try.*

*We may be willing to negotiate and say we'll stay in remis-
sion for a while, praying that it doesn't come back. Because that's
the other thing. Once, once you acknowledge the harms, and you
fix it to the degree you can, what do you do to ensure that it
doesn't come back to harm future generations?*

Fisher-Stewart's response follows in the line of a kind of
measured expectation of what's achievable that I've found common among Black people engaged in this work. For Christians,
that measured expectation stands in tension with the fact that
we call ourselves a death and resurrection people: we hold up
the hope of a final, definitive redemption. We proclaim that
God's grace will dry every tear and make all things whole. I was
curious how Fisher-Stewart navigates the space between tran-
scendent hopes and pragmatic assessments of what's possible:

*We talk about resurrection, but no one's trying to rush to get it.
So a lot of times we talk a good game but we're not trying to figure it out. We're not trying to get there to see if this thing called
resurrection really works. But I think once you have the listing
of harms, and I don't know how many things are on that list,
but we'll see it, and say, "Oh crap," and there will be a necessary
reckoning.*

*Let's take racial self-hatred. Black folks don't want to do a
lot of stuff that's Black. We don't want rituals or traditions that
are African in our churches. Not even Africans Anglicans want
to do it. They want it British, they want it Anglican. But they
don't want it African. Once you put that out there, then you
ask, where did you learn to hate yourselves, your traditions,
your cultures?*

*We were told we were no good. We were criminals. We're not
white. We could never be intelligent. We have taken that in ourselves, and it manifests itself in that in our churches, we want to*

be as white as possible. To some degree, we want to look as white as possible.

Hearing those words hurt. Because I knew that, whereas historically my people have often falsely taken credit for other culture's ideas, the internalized racism Black people experience is in fact not something they came up with on their own. Racialized self-hatred may be the only thing we can definitely say white folks actually taught Black people. As I thought about this, I remembered something I'd heard Fisher-Stewart say regarding reparations. It was something I'd heard my colleague and wife, Rondesia Jarrett-Schell, also say, almost word for word: "I don't want a single cent for any of you. I just want to be left alone."

Given that history of indoctrinating self-hatred, I had to wonder whether, if we ever did the kind of reckoning Fisher-Stewart proposed, we would discover that every time we, that is white people, engage with Black people, we only make things worse, that we only ever do harm. And if that is so, then, maybe the best we could offer would be to acknowledge that we're only going to make this worse, and so, step back and make space. And maybe that's the most we could hope for in terms of reparations. I suggested this to Fisher-Stewart. She smiled wryly before answering:

> *There's something about white people. Sometimes you think you know everything. When you come into a situation, you assume you have all the answers.*
>
> *Let's take this thing Rondesia and I both said. We were both speaking from a personal perspective. But we also have to look at our people, beyond ourselves. There may be some of our folk who do need a check.*
>
> *We can go and look at the Episcopal schools and whether or not our Black kids could attend them. And if they had been able to attend them, would they be in a better position now as adults?*

Maybe. So we'll offer scholarships. We can't fix things for the folks who were shut out before. But we can make it so if there's any Black child who wants to attend an Episcopal school, who does not have the funds, that they will have the funds to attend now, so that future generations have that opportunity.

The point Fisher-Stewart raises here is essential. Whatever form reparations make take, they must point toward the future, and build opportunities for those that follow, for those who are still to come. Sometimes, this is as much about tearing down roadblocks as it is about building new bridges:

It's not an either/or, it's a both. And a big part of it is eliminating obstacles and that's where Rondesia and I were going. It wasn't so much "leave us alone;" as "just get out of our way." I'll be able to do for myself, If you just get out of my way, if you just stop putting obstacles in my way. As we look around the Episcopal Church, there are so many obstacles. I'm hearing more and more about the ordination process for Black folks.

I was at an event recently, and it was amazing. All these white people came in and they had just been baptized "yesterday" and they're in the ordination process. And you think, "How in the world did this happen?" When I know Black folks trying for ten years to get through the ordination process. Let's ask that question. Let's look at that, to ask why is it some white person who just popped in over here is at the front of the line?

Identifying these roadblocks, and removing them is no trivial thing. Racism has adapted. It's gotten clever. We code it carefully now. These days racialized obstacles are built looking like race-blind policies. Those of us who are white might not even notice the racialized nature of the policies we've created, and operate in. So we have to dig deep, and question foundational assumptions we've taken for granted. In predominantly white Christian churches, we need to interrogate a whole host of practices and traditions and ask, "Is this actually the Gospel, or is it just whiteness?" Fisher-Stewart gives the example of the Episcopal Church's nominally race-blind ordination process.

> *We've got these ordination exams, right? Tests you have to pass to be ordained. The questions are biased against people of color. Then there is the Commission on Ministry. I have a Latina colleague who went before her COM, and they asked a question about spiritual disciplines in worship: what practices do you use to make worship spiritually engaged? She mentioned that she uses sage. And the COM members went crazy. She was marked down on her assessment because she says, "I use sage before I pray: I open the windows and I sage the room." Well, what is the difference between that and incense?*
>
> *We get blocked out of opportunities, because we don't give you your answer, but we give you an answer based on our culture and our traditions. That doesn't mean our answers are wrong. It just means they're different. As the Reverend Jeremiah Wright says, "It's just different, not deficient." And is the Church willing to acknowledge differences throughout the church? Not just on certain occasions, but foundationally.*

As I think about reparations now, I believe the kind of foundational shift Gayle Fisher-Stewart describes as an essential component. That said, I'll still tell any white church that listens they need to surrender 15%.

CHAPTER

8

Evaluation

The process of confessions, repentance, repair and reconciliation is always ongoing. Even when considering the
course of our individual and personal repentance, it's clear
most of us struggle with the same sins, over and over again. Our
efforts at repentance are influenced by the very sin we hope to
leave behind. Predominantly white institutions cannot simply
quit white supremacy in a single decision and act of will. It will
continue to shape up, despite our best efforts to be rid of it. Even
our attempts toward anti-racist agitation, will be influenced by
centuries of white supremacist culture, catechism, and formation
that still mold our thinking. This is not cause for despair. It is reason to commit to a continual process of evaluation, accountability,
and repentance, so that we can grow toward the sort of church
Jesus wants us to be.

The Episcopal Church's baptismal covenant provides a
helpful and concise framework for what this looks like, and
how it works:

> *Celebrant* Will you persevere in resisting evil, and, when-
> ever you fall into sin, repent and return to the
> Lord?
> *People* I will, with God's help.

In its brevity the question clarifies four essential principles
regarding the process of repentance.

First, we commit to persevere in resisting evil. That is, we do our level best to walk free from the influence of sin.

Second, we acknowledge the inevitable fact that we will fall into sin. Note that the question states "*whenever* you fall into sin," not "*if* we fall into sin."

Third, we prepare ourselves in advance to acknowledge the fault, and repent, striving to do better, whenever it comes up.

Finally, we admit we need help to continue in this walk of repentance. And so we say, "with God's help." With respect to reparations initiatives, and more generally to the efforts of predominantly white institutions to repent of white supremacy, this means instituting policies and procedures that anticipate (and embrace) conflict, while working to evaluate and improve our efforts at anti-racist action.

In our conversations, I've come to admire how Knapper's thinking blends principled compassion, incisive practicality, and creative vision. Anyone aspiring to take on reparations should strive to emulate this. In that spirit, Knapper clarifies the need to establish structures that anticipate conflict:

> *Create an avenue to deal with conflict at the beginning: both internally and externally.*
>
> *When you are creating a space intended to deal with the many ways our systems harm us, every day, all of the time, that is going to bring in certain levels of disagreement and conflict.*
>
> *Waiting for potential harm, waiting until conflict and harm happen, before you think of a way to deal with it, is, in itself harmful. In many of the spaces I've been in the past, when there have been situations of harm or conflict, there was no shared agreement amongst the group working together on how we would deal with conflict when it pops up.*

In many of these institutions there is already a power imbalance that's very much built into the fabric of the institution. If you're not intentionally thinking about that, before the deep work starts, then the work itself will be vulnerable to falling apart and unraveling when people get lost and unable to move through conflict.

That's something that I recommend doing right at the start, in any space where I'm working, but particularly in spaces doing deep work that's centered on dealing with harm. You need to think about how you will deal with conflict internally as a group with one another, and also, how will you deal with conflict that comes from outside sources?

It's important to draft a core set of values that are created collectively, and center whatever vulnerable community you are looking to create repair with, or support for, or work alongside with. You need to check that your values center that community, or those communities, and check that with every decision that you make, you are visiting those values and asking the question like: "How does this connect with the values that we created together?" Does this live up to the values that we have agreed to uphold together?

And if the answer is that it doesn't, you need to be okay with taking a pause, revisiting the decision, and figuring out where this went wrong, not just moving forward for the sake of time.

Drawing again from the words of the baptismal covenant, and our commitment to "strive to resist evil," we must first strive to ensure our efforts and initiatives are free from the white supremacist practices that have defined our institutions. This is why Knapper advises drafting a statement of core values and objectives for your reparations work early on, and returning to it at every decision point, to determine whether or not we are in line with the goals and values we have set for ourselves.

This process demands commitment to internal work; interrogating the many ways structures of whiteness have shaped our assumptions and perceptions. It requires a disciplined commitment to center the leadership, authority, perspective and insight of those most directly impacted by the system of white supremacy we aim to address and challenge, specifically the Black and brown folk living in and around our own institutions. As Knapper cautions, it requires a focused determination to move with all the urgency of human need, while refusing to act in haste for the sake of efficiency, or "getting it done."

> *I like to say that it's important that we move with urgency, and understand that when we delay the movement of progress that it has very real effect on people's lives. Moving with urgency is incredibly important.*
>
> *But I also think that we shouldn't move with the speed of capitalism: We shouldn't move forward without intention, without care, without being thoughtful about why we are doing the things we do. If it takes time that is okay. We shouldn't conflate urgency with just wanting to get a thing out of the way.*
>
> *Which happens a lot in advocacy spaces. People just want to get the bill passed. People just want to get the thing built, or the project finished. People want to check these things off as completed without stopping to think: "Why are we doing this? How are we doing this?" Because how does matter. It's not just the end result. Because in the end, people will be impacted by how it was done.*
>
> *Checking in with your values is one of the most important things you can do when you're collectively building toward doing something huge: breaking the systems of harm that exist.*

We must strive for this level of intentionality at all times.

And we must acknowledge we will fall short. We will be blindsided by our own biases. At times we will fall into the traps of white paternalism. We will not always center the leadership of those with the most skin in the game. We will rush, skip ahead and do damage in our haste.

If we don't acknowledge this at the front end, if we don't prepare ourselves for these shortcomings and warning signs, we are likely to blow right by them, not notice where we have gone astray, and continue in our missteps.

Some care is necessary here. Simply stating "sometimes we're going to be unconsciously racist," helps no one at all. Such statements can end up being an excuse, as if these patterns were inevitable. They are not. These statements can also become sinkholes of neurotic guilt: trapping us to wallow in the sin of our racism rather than move beyond it.

In setting up the expectation of falling short along the way, our objective should be to push toward healthy guilt, the kind of guilt that acknowledges the offenses, asserts that is within our ability to better, and focuses on the actions we can take to improve. This is precisely the ethos of repentance, of returning to our core values, of returning to our Lord.

The people's response to the questions of the baptismal covenant, "I will with God's help," conveys both our commitment to the continual and ongoing process of repentance, and also our acknowledgment that we cannot do it alone. When I speak the words "with God's help" I often imagine some disembodied, ethereal, and supernatural force, invisibly boosting and bolstering my will.

The trouble with this understanding is that it can be difficult to discern how God's strength is working inside us. It is seductively easy to confuse God's strength, which works in line with God's purposes, with our own will, which works in line with what we want. And what we want, usually, is to be reassured that everything we're doing is just fine.

Institutionally, this tendency means that internal evaluation of our racial justice and reparations efforts will be biased toward confirming that we've achieved our objectives. Two practices help avoid this tendency.

The first is the simple matter of setting clear targets, timeliness, and periods for evaluation from the outset. This makes it easy to measure our efforts and our success. Churches are often hesitant to do this. We prefer to feel our way forward through a field of mushy, ill-defined, goals.

Every so often, I get invited to a church or other institution to talk about this work. I always ask the same questions before agreeing: "What do you hope to achieve with our time together?" and "How will you know if we've accomplished it?" Most of the time, people tell me these are great questions. Just as often, they struggle to answer them.

I suspect some of this difficulty is conditioned by our protestant sensibilities around the importance of grace. We talk about "not putting a period where God put a common," or "making room for the Holy Spirit." But Jesus tells us the Holy Spirit goes where She chooses. She does not require our permission. She does not need us to make space. She takes care of that.

Stating clear targets and timelines for reparation does not preclude us from revising or changing course entirely, if it becomes clear that is what God's grace demands. Setting measurable goals is not about closing off the horizon of possibility, it's just about making sure we don't just wander in circles. As C. Michael Livingston, a lay leader at my congregation, often reminds me: "we must have a plan to deviate from."

The second practice that helps avoid the trap of self-satisfied evaluation is to plan and provide for external criticism.

When we read scripture, it's clear that God's preferred mode of pulling us toward repentance is prophetic, that is, through the witness of people with whom we are in relationship. Read this question of the baptismal covenant again: *"Will you persevere in resisting evil, and, whenever you fall into sin, repent and return to the Lord?"*

The question implies that we will notice when we fall into sin. This isn't always the case. More often than not, we feel justified in our own sins, especially if they show up in pursuit of a just cause, something like reparations for the legacy of anti-Black racism. We need, and we depend, on others to show us the fault. Of course, this ties back to the first step, building relationships. The partnerships of accountability you have already built will be where you gather, when your timelines and targets are complete, to look back, to consider whether you've actually what you set out to accomplish, and to decide where to go next. You may find you need to stop, go back and change course. Throughout the work of the Reparations Task Force, Fisher-Stewart has been our internal voice of accountability and conscience.

> *As we go down the track I have to stop and ask some questions and so I can keep going on with you. And it's going to be like that. We'll do the work, and then we'll have to ask more questions. To me, it seems like our process is more in depth than others, because they're too quick to come to the answer. They want to say we've solved it.*
>
> *I've heard some folks in Maryland are upset because they're giving out checks, and people are asking, "Okay, so what does this do?" What are you repairing? What harms did the Episcopal Church cause? Or is it just, pay the check, say we did reparations, and move on to something else?*

You're really taking them through their paces, Peter. This has been a long process. Because I remember how you thought you had the amount figured out three years ago, and that you could just go to the diocese and say, "Here is the bill, we have to pay it." Somebody said "Oh, crap. He's figured it out. And we've got how many Black parishes? Let's write this check and divvy it up." But you didn't let it rest at that. This has been a lot of work. And it also just shows us how much more work there is to do.

Because these stages of reparation are a cycle, not a journey with an endpoint. Ayers articulates the hope that we could be transformed through this work, and become a repairing people, seeking out all the harms that still remain hidden, bringing them to light, and doing what whatever is within our power to make them right.

My biggest hope is that we become a people that looks for harms to repair. We almost get addicted to repairing harms. So it doesn't become what you're talking about, people saying we did it, we're done, we did a cash transfer, problem solved. Instead, we're looking and digging and saying like, "Who else have we hurt? Who else needs repair?"

If you talk to a couples therapist, they'll tell you people get stuck thinking apologies fix everything. People will think "Well I said, I was sorry. What else do you want from me?" We don't want that kind of mentality, because apologies don't fix everything. We want the kind of mentality that says: "What else can I do to ensure I'm not exploiting anybody?" And I don't want that to be misconstrued. I don't mean to say that it's never enough. But I do hope that we're eager to be a people that owns our mistakes, and then asks, "How can we make up for it?"

That posture of humility could transform our entire country. Especially here, because we're the epicenter, DC is cap. We're the capital, the center point for so much of what this country looks to do. If we had a posture of saying: "We are going to do our best to find the harms, and fix the harms and not settle for saying, 'We've done it, move on,'" I think we'd see that ripple effect.

9

Forgiveness, Absolution?

W hen I talk with other white people about reparations, almost without fail, someone will ask, "When does forgiveness come into the process?"

I understand the impulse and longing behind this question. I share in it. When we recognize that we have participated in, and benefited from, the sabotage of another human being, or worse still, of an entire people, we feel the weight of that debt pressing down. We ache to be free of it. If you're white like me, you probably just want some person of color to tell you it's okay, to tell you you're okay. This impulse is natural. Nonetheless, we must put it aside.

Forwarding our need for forgiveness and absolution is counterproductive on two fronts. First, it makes our absolution, rather than the repair of harms we have participated in, the focus of the work. This focus will condition and shape all the decisions we make.

My Grandmother once told me, "If you're looking for forgiveness, you're not ready to say, 'I'm sorry.'" On the surface, her statement appears oxymoronic. In general conversation we use the phrases "ask forgiveness" and "apologize," almost interchangeably. But in fact, the two actions are entirely different.

Asking forgiveness speaks to my need to be unburdened from guilt I feel.

If I'm asking for absolution, I will do whatever is necessary to get you to say the words "I forgive you," whether or not you mean them, or want to offer them. Once the words are offered, it's likely I will consider the matter settled, and wander off with a free conscience. If it turns out you haven't actually forgiven me despite the words I coerced, if you come back to me and say, "This still hurts," there's a good chance I'll blame you for bringing it up again, or tell you to get over it. I might demand to know why you can't forgive me for it.

In short, asking for forgiveness prioritizes the needs of those who've done harm over and against the needs of those who have been harmed. All too often, this dynamic governs our conversations around race in this country.

By contrast, apology, confession, and repentance focus on the harm that has been committed and the person who has been harmed. Apology says, "I recognize I hurt you. I regret that I did. What can I do to help make it right? Because I want you to be well."

Thus, if you're looking for forgiveness, you're not ready to say, "I'm sorry," because you are still centering your own needs over those of the person you've harmed. To the extent that the needs of the aggressor should show up in apology at all, it is only with the statement "I don't want to be someone who hurts my neighbor."

The second reason that forwarding forgiveness is counterproductive to reparation is that the demand for forgiveness can actually be a further injury to the people we have harmed. Demanding forgiveness can be, for some, another example of people of color being required to put aside their own emotional needs, in order to tend to the emotional needs of whites.

There is real pressure behind this push for forgiveness. I suspect most white people and most predominantly white institutions carry at least a subconscious awareness of the racist hardships we've participated in and benefited from. And, like adulterers who constantly suspect their spouses of cheating, we wonder, and fear, if people of color might decide to return these wounds in kind. We want to hear words of forgiveness from Black and brown folk, so that we don't have to worry about it anymore.

This worry and anxiety can manifest reactively against people of color who refuse to make a show of forgiveness and reconciliation. Black and brown folk who show visible resentment for the racist hurts they experience can find themselves shunned, professionally sabotaged, or subject to violence. That is to say, when whites ask for forgiveness, there can be negative repercussions for Black and brown folk who refuse to offer it. The ask, and the expectation itself, are dangerous.

I don't mean to belittle the idea of forgiveness. Forgiveness can be powerful and liberatory for both offender and offended. It can release us from the wounds and injuries of the past. It *can* do those things, but it doesn't *always*. And forgiveness never accomplishes anything if it's coerced. The victim alone has the right to offer forgiveness. or not.

We understand this intuitively in our worship and sacraments. We confess our sins. We commit to repent. But it is God's choice whether we will be forgiven or not. We can't compel it. We have no right to demand it.

Similarly, white people and white institutions have no right to expect forgiveness from the people who have been harmed by the racist practices we take part in. Some people of color will choose to forgive. That is their right. Some will choose not to. That is also their right. There can be no legitimate moral judgment on this choice one way or the other. If forgiveness is offered, we can receive it as a grace. And if not, that must be okay too.

This point is crucial. If we are serious about making repair, we must release our expectation of forgiveness entirely. With regard to reparations, we should excise all language of forgiveness from our mission statements, our progress reports, and resolutions. We must prepare ourselves for the possibility that, even after unearthing and confessing all the harms, even after making restitution to the fullest extent it is possible, the communities we have harmed might still choose not to forgive. They might still choose not to be reconciled. And we must be willing to accept this fact. Knapper lays this out very clearly.

> *You need to know that even if you do all of these things, even if you go through the process of giving back, of shifting wealth to communities, that it's been stolen from, at the end of the day. that community may still be very angry with you, and it may not change how they look at you at all. And you're just going to have to be okay with it. That community still doesn't owe you any-thing. They don't owe you a thank you, or friendship or kinship.*
>
> *Reparations can be a way to create repair, by which we may be able to move toward those things. But you're not owed those things. Once white people can accept and understand that, and make that the process in which they live their lives, then so many of these other things will come so much easier.*

If we are not willing to undertake the work of reparations for its own sake, for the sake of those who have been harmed, then perhaps we should not undertake it at all. Because if we won't make reparation for the simple rightness of it, then as my grandmother might say, we're just not ready to say we're sorry.

And we're likely to cause more harm in the attempt. If nothing else, we could be honest about that fact.

Even to whatever extent forgiveness or reconciliation enter the process, they may show up in ways that challenge our expectations and hope. Years ago, Fisher-Stewart offered simple operational definition of forgiveness that I still wrestle with today:

> *Forgiveness means I won't do to you what you did to me. That's it.*

This is not the kudos and hugs vision of forgiveness so many of us long for. But it is real, and honest. It respects and cares for both the injured and those who caused injury. And it may be the most we can hope for.

We may also need to moderate our hopes for what reconciliation looks like. It might not be the racial melting pot, salad, rainbow or whatever grand metaphor we were taught in elementary school. It might be something far humbler, more pragmatic, and still more profound. Baxter offers one vision for what it might look like:

> *I think we should see more interactions and partnerships between Black churches and white churches, more like sister churches. It would be especially good to see congregations that are strong on their finances partnering with Black congregations that may not be as strong financially. If they could find a way to partner together, in a sense that's reconciliation and the work of reparations. I would love to see that.*
>
> *I'd like to see more interactions between congregations overall, throughout the diocese, but also as a community, amongst Black churches as well. Too many Black churches in the Diocese of Washington have been siloed, instead of coming together in*

community and talking about what changes need to be made, and what work needs to be done together. That would be part of reconciliation as well, when you consider where and how different Black churches were founded, often along lines of the splits over the racial issue.

It is possible we may never be one. It may be that unity is not even to be desired. But with repentance, reformation and reparation, we might just be able to live as neighbors with justice, equity and respect. That might be enough.

10

Resources for Perseverance

As we've seen, taking the path of reparations is a long-term commitment. It is difficult, humbling work. It requires acknowledging missteps along the way, changing and adjusting course, surrendering and sacrifice. At some point, you will almost certainly want to give up. Or perhaps you'll just quietly step back and let the work fall by the way.

The history of reparations has been a history of broken promises, from General Sherman's special field order #15, and its commitment of forty acres and mule, on down into the present. If we don't want to add to that history, if we don't want to find ourselves unintentionally compounding the racist hurts of the past, we must find the wherewithal to continue forward. Mere willpower will not be enough. You and your reparations working community will need to align resources and strategies to sustain you along the way. I ask each of the conversation partners you've met in this book what sustains them in the work they do. As you'll see, their answers varied widely. And yet, there was set of core themes and resources that showed up throughout. Within your working group, you'll want to think about how you hold and provide these resources for one another. These core resources for perseverance are:

1. Knowing Your Skin in the Game
2. A Community of Support
3. Spiritual Grounding
4. Humility and Growth Mindset

I'll describe each one briefly, while letting our conversation partners fill out the details.

1. Knowing Your Skin in the Game

You need to know why you're doing this work of reparations. You need to know why you're willing to put in the time, to open yourself up to criticism and correction, to be humbled along the way. You need to be able to say why it matters to you. And just saying, "It's the right thing to do," probably won't cut it.

I take it as a given that we all act out of self-interest. Neurologists teach us that our brains are reward seeking organs. Jesus himself speaks in the language of self-interest even, and especially when he calls us to acts of transgressive compassion. "Love your enemies, and pray for those who persecute you," he tells us, before adding: "so that you will be children of God." The centrality of self-interest doesn't preclude empathy, compassion or sacrifice. It just means acknowledging that we all have reasons for the choices we make. We get something out of it. That something will be different for different people. But, if you can't name that, you'll have a hard time carrying through to the end.

Schulken can speak with specificity to the stake she has in this work:

There are two things that have drawn me to the work. One is my immediate family. My family is racially mixed. I'm white. My son's white. My daughter's Asian, and she's now eighteen. So, for the last eighteen years, I've been exploring what that means. What does it mean to be a racially mixed family in the U.S.? What does it mean to have a daughter who has experiences in this world that I don't have? She's adopted, and the post-adoption services we've received tend to focus more on adoption issues and less on racial issues. There's definitely another piece of work I'd like to be doing around the issues of race and ethics in the adoption industry.

Regardless, part of my interest in this has come from within my family. I've had to come to a realization of my own whiteness, of what it's like for a person of color to grow up in a white family and navigate whiteness. I've had to work on that.

A lot of adoptive parents in the DC metro area, when talking about transracial adoption, will start with the line, "Well, we live in a diverse area," as if we deserve brownie points for that. Hey, I used to say exactly the same thing. But I learned that's not enough to help your child figure out their racial identity and navigate whiteness. You can't just plop people of color into a diverse area without doing the work yourself. I knew I had to do better than that.

I can't say the moment that I realized I needed to do more work on this. It's been a gradual process of learning one thing after another. That's one part of what drew me to the reparations work.

Committed relationships of care, love and attention can be a crucial source of motivation and accountability for this work. But we must also work to develop our internal drives for the work. We need to know what personal skin we have in the game. That question often comes down to a question of self-understanding. Schulken talks about what this looks like:

> *The other part is my ancestral history. I've known since I was a little kid that my great-great grandfather was an enslaver. As I've done more research, I have found twelve ancestors who were also enslavers. That's a lot of cruelty, a lot of inhumanity. Growing up in the South, that was not considered a bad thing. I was brought up in white supremacy. My grandparents had Black servants whom I adored, but who were not allowed to join us for the meals they prepared for us or even enter the house through the front door. When integration actually started in North Carolina, fourteen years after* Brown v. Board of Education, *my brother and I were sent to a white flight segregation academy. I was steeped in the Lost Cause.*
>
> *Coming out of that was a gradual process too. When I left home and went to college, when I moved away from North Carolina, I started trying to learn the truth of what's really going around us. Because I grew up with a whole bunch of fantasy. Whether it was the way we taught our history, or things we learned in church, these fantasies of white supremacy pervaded everything that I grew up with. Coming out of it was a process.*

It is okay if you're still working out this question. But you'll need to keep reaching for it. Schulken can name some pieces of what drives her, but there are other parts she's still searching out.

> *I feel like I owe it to my daughter to help her navigate this world, and as a white woman, I'm not really well qualified to do that. So I need to work on it. But it's tricky sometimes to figure out for ourselves why we're doing this. In part, it's just because telling the truth is the right thing to do. I don't have a lot of tolerance for lies. And I might still be rebelling, like a teenager or something.*

Everything I've learned is all the polar opposite of everything that I grew up with and everything I was taught.

But on some level, I don't know why I keep pushing. There is this drive in me to just keep digging.

Your sense of skin in the game may come from your identity: you may understand this work to be part of your calling. Ayers, a lawyer, working with a secular organization, nonetheless describes her vocation with a clarity of calling that I have rarely heard from any priest:

When I first started at DC Justice Lab in the fall, I definitely felt it was something God wanted for me personally. I have to put a disclaimer out, that DC Justice Lab is not a faith-based organization. But I am a believer. When I started, I was planning on doing primarily criminal records sealing. But Patrice kept mentioning that she really needed someone to take over reparations. I sat down and prayed about it. And the Lord said, "That's you." And I was like "Me? Why?" He started to highlight my personal connection to it, my own family history. And I thought, "If the Lord has highlighted this for me, then I really need to see what he has to say about it."

Sometimes we hear the Lord's voice in the witness of those who walked the road ahead of us. There's nothing wrong with looking toward others for personal inspiration and guidance. In fact, it shows admirable wisdom.

So I read "Reparations: A Christian Call for Repentance and Repair" by Duke Kwon, a pastor here in DC. It seemed almost too perfect: he's a Christian, here in DC, and he's talking about reparations.

I dove into that book, and was blown away at the Biblical explanation of how we handle harms that have been done.

Regardless of when those harms were committed, if we become aware of them, and they have not been made right, then it is our job, regardless of where we fall in the lineage, to make it right for the descendants of those who were harmed, whoever they may be. The breakdown that he provided in the scriptures and the biblical context he provided gave me a strong framework to look at how God addresses and views harm. I could see how God views the person that is engaging in harm and what they need to do; and how God views the person that is the recipient of harm and what they need to do.

Working toward reparations requires facing a history of deep trauma and abuse, and then returning to it again and again. It's hard not to become callous and disillusioned. So alongside the fires that inspire us, and strengthen us, we need to find the wells that will help us stay receptive and empathetic. Ayers holds both these gifts in admirable measure:

As I'm going into this work, I think my faith has kept me from becoming hard hearted. They'll joke at work that I'm always the first to cry when we talk about what's happening under our three branches of policing, prosecution or punishment. But I'm grateful the Lord has given me that verse from Ephesians 4:32, as a life verse for me: "Be kind and tender hearted with one another, forgiving each other as Christ has forgiven you."

I don't think you can read about the horrors of slavery, or the immense and painful discrimination that has occurred in our country, the redlining, the housing discrimination, the lynchings, the abuse, the bombings, and the burnings and not become hardhearted without the Lord. He's kept me tender-hearted to not see people as the sin, but to see the sin as the sin, to disengage it from the person and not make it their identity. That can be tough when you are reading about the same sin, over and over, and the same group of people committing it. It's not an easy feat.

I'm not perfect at that. But, because I'm not, I do a lot of intercession and prayer over both groups. It gives me a place to lament. And I do lament, you see me tearing up right now. I lament, and I grieve and pray over the fact that all of us, knowingly and unknowingly are carrying around generational trauma, regardless of "what side" our ancestors were on. There's still trauma that's coming through that bloodline. There's still beliefs and expectations and, and distrust of each other that's coming through.

I'm just constantly in prayer asking "God to show me, what does healing look like in the city? What does repair look like in the city? What does love look like on display in this city? And how can I be an agent for that and a light for that?"

It's an interesting intersection: I need to occupy that cerebral space to craft something legal around this, but also hold that emotional space to stay, and the spiritual space to stay grounded. It's a lot. I wouldn't wish this on anybody. But I'm grateful for it.

Your sense of calling to this work may show up in a much more pragmatic and immanent way. Fisher Stewart expresses her commitment to the Task Force as a clear understanding that someone must ask the tough questions, and if not her, then who?

What keeps me with the Task Force? The same thing that keeps me in the Christian church, and that keeps me in the Episcopal Church. On a moment's notice, I could just say I'm done. I don't need any of this. I can find Jesus at the beach. I don't need to call myself anything other than a follower of Jesus.

But what keeps me on the Task Force is that someone needs to ask the difficult questions. And so I listen. And I throw a little question and say okay, let me see what happens with that one. And it is not to keep people on the straight and narrow. I just want to get us to open our minds: What if we do it this way? Have you thought about this? Have you considered this perspective?

Most fundamentally, have you really put yourself in my shoes? The Task Force is a very white group. Most of the time it's just me, and maybe an occasional Black person passing through. And my question is, have you ever tried to put yourself in my place, just being in this group, listening to you discuss me, and my people, and what you're going to do for us, and how you're going to do for us?

That's hard. But then if all the Black folk just said we're out of here, then nothing, nothing, nothing would ever happen. So that keeps me at the table. To kind of ask those tough questions, to get you to think it through.

Knowing Fisher-Stewart, I think there is also a fundamental drive in her character that pushes toward, and perhaps even enjoys, asking the questions everyone else is trying to ignore. The fact that you're reading a book on reparations suggests you might have a similar inclination. If you do have it, it's a tremendous asset. If that's your drive for this work, lean hard into it. Because those uncomfortable questions may reveal what can actually be accomplished:

For me the toughest question, and it's not rhetorical, it's a real question is this: Is the diocese really serious about this? The Committee, or the Task Force might come up with an actual dollar amount for reparations. And if we're honest about what that is, the diocese might answer "Whoa, whoa, whoa, that will break us."

Well, okay. You have to risk something to gain something.

But we don't know if our congregations have the will to take that risk. We need to survey our congregations to find out if they actually care about reparations. Because if folks don't care about it, if it is not on their radar, and they're just happy with what's going on, they're not going to do anything.

You know, if we had 50% of the 88 congregations doing something about repair, we'd be really doing something. But I don't even think it comes close to 50% doing the real hard work.

And those that are doing something, how substantial is it? They might have an Absalom Jones service or, something for Black history, and something for women's history, and Indigenous people's history. But are they really ready to change, to look at themselves and say, why are we like this? Because reparation will require real change. And if you ask the question, many congregations would answer, "No. We like things the way they are."

Whatever your self-interest in this work, you must be able to name it. Because at some point, amidst all the frustrations and setbacks, after hearing people respond: "We like things the way they are," one time too many, you will ask yourself, "Why am I doing this?" And you will need to have an answer ready. If you're still struggling to figure that out, let me share one beautiful grace you may find along the way, if you persevere, from Knapper. While they are rightly and appropriately focused on the resources for creative restoration and care that reparations could represent to Black and brown communities, they also acknowledge that process of accountability presents the hope of healing for white people too:

Reparation is part of the infrastructure of care. I recently rewatched the James Baldwin film, I Am Not Your Negro. One of the things that Baldwin talks about is how we have a responsibility to look at the life around us, and to see what

*our place is in it, and what our responsibility is to each other.
Reparations gives an opportunity, a powerful opportunity, to
those who have benefited off of these harms, to be able to be part
of this infrastructure of care. It gives them an opportunity to be
part of a moral repair within themselves. I think that is such a
gift, if it's something that you can embrace.*

2. A Community of Support

Especially when you are engaging in work that can be humbling, internally challenging and frustrating, you need a group
of people who will see the good in you, and remind you of it.
This is very different from the people you may know who are
always blowing smoke up where the sun doesn't shine. This is
not a community of cheerleaders. These are the people who
recognize, name, and will hold you to the best of yourself.
Imani offers a powerful testimony to the community that both
supports her and keeps her accountable.

*When I went off to college, it was the first time I'd been on my
own. I was recently talking to this sister I knew from that period.
And she was saying how, when we were getting to know each
other in college, she heard things about me, awful things, that
didn't match up with her experience of me. I remembered that.
I'd never been maligned that way before. It's easy to get swayed
by that kind of thing. You find yourself tempted to go along to get
along. You have to learn to march to the beat of your own drum-
mer. And hope you find people who want to join the band.*

*It helps knowing you belong to people, and knowing specif-
ically who you belong to. I've got communities. I come from family. I got a church community. I got a college community. I got a
graduate school community. Wherever I go, I've got community. I
belong to them, and I'm responsible to them.*

I know that whatever happens in my life, no matter what I do, if I get strung out addicted to crack, or whatever, I could go to Nashville, and find at least fifteen doorsteps that I could show up on, without warning, needing help, and I'd get it.

Developing this kind of communal support provides comfort and encouragement, but also a galvanizing sense of accountability:

So I don't fear the rejection or judgment of these institutions. I belong to people, and they show up for me. So, for their sake, I cannot lie. I can't. I cannot add to the truth when I go out into the world, because I carry my family's name, and my community's name. I don't get to play games like somebody who doesn't belong to anybody. It's a double-sided thing. They show up for me. I have to show up for them. That's all.

Before I got my professional training, when I was at Howard, I was so grateful to study under Dr. Elizabeth Clark-Lewis. When I was a student there, she really hit hard, instilling this sense that we were only there because somebody busted their butt for us to get to that position. So, we don't get, and we don't want, the luxury of being individualistic. We can't get stuck in that conspicuous consumption: that attitude of "get your money, pussyfoot around, don't speak truth to power, don't advocate for your communities," just so you can get that one big house in that one nice neighborhood.

Your community of support may not be a singular group. Schulken paints the picture of a community of support she pulled together from several places in her life.

A big part of what sustains me is the fellowship of others who are doing this work: for example this group, the Reparations Task Force, or the members of my church involved in racial justice, or my dear next-door neighbor. He's a white man who left the Catholic priesthood to marry a Black woman forty-seven years ago, not long after Loving v. Virginia. I've spent many years learning from him. We share stories all the time of what we've learned about ourselves—and our whiteness—from the people we love who are not white.

Your community of support may be a place where you can find respite, simply to be yourself and be affirmed as you are. This is particularly important when the work may be calling your self-identity into question. The context is different, but nonetheless, Baxter speaks to this aspect of self-affirmation when he describes what he loves about the Black church:

What I love about the Black church is you can be unapologetically Black. The Black church has its issues, and there are reforms that need to be done within. But again, it is a place where you can be unapologetically Black. You can be your authentic self.

It's a place where you can come, and share in community your, share your joys and your struggles. When you have this history of dealing with racism, it's a place where you can come together in solidarity, and really see who you are, see the image of God in you, and not the image of what society tries to define you to be. It's a place where you can see that you matter, not only to other people, but also to God, despite what the larger society may say, or try and cast upon you.

I believe in the power of the Black church, and the work it's being called to do. There are some things we need to step out and do differently in the 21st century. But I deeply believe, when you look at what the Black church did to sustain people through some of the most tremendous and horrific periods of history, you get a sense of what we can still do, if we get back on that same accord again, for our community that's being ravaged by new challenges today: gun violence, drugs and the affordable housing crunch. We can overcome these as well. We've shown it. The Black church has shown its ability to change the course of a nation. I think we will be able to do that again.

3. Spiritual Grounding

Of course, as a priest and evangelist I like to share the story of what faith has done for me. But it may be that, despite its title, there are some secular or skeptical folk reading this book, searching for insight for their own organization's reparations process. So I will frame this question more broadly. You need to know where to find the wells that sustain you, whether you think of them religiously or not. Where do you go for restoration and rejuvenation when it seems the world seems dry? Find those places and go back to them frequently. Ayers highlighted the importance of self-care and prayer when I asked her how she endures in this work:

> *Prayer. Like anybody else I have my moments when I think "I don't see where I'm making a difference." If anybody tells you they never felt that way, they're either lying or delusional. I don't know which one.*
>
> *It's definitely hard. I couldn't do this without prayer. It gives me time to reflect and see what I need to do; to be able to adapt, and center myself.*
>
> *Self-care matters too. No one wants you to make space for yourself to regenerate. But you can't do this work if you don't take that time.*

That spiritual grounding offers not only restoration and reserves to continue on, but provides perspective to overcome the frustrations, and often, down-right nonsense, you may encounter when pursuing reparations. As Imani relates it:

> *You've got to be clean in your own walk, and stick by your own devotions, to keep your integrity. I spend a lot of time with God, asking God to guide my understanding and clarify what is my work, and what is my calling, and what is my duty? You've got to have an internal register for those things to keep your integrity.*
>
> *It is hard. You've got to be fearless. That's where faith comes in. It gives you that groundedness to check and make sure your ego isn't driving the car. To be sure that if you're given the chance to do right by people, you will do it. You'll still show up professionally, because after all, these organizations hired you to be a professional. But you won't make it about yourself.*

I think we, and here I mean Christians in particular, often misunderstand humility. We think of humility putting us in a posture of compliance. But the kind of humility Imani describes, the kind that checks to make sure our ego isn't driving the car, engenders a certain boldness. Because in realizing, and owning that this work does not depend on us alone, we recognize that it does not depend on anyone else alone either. And this is important because undertaken reparations will often involve engaging institutions that habitually believe they hold final and ultimate authority in the matter. Imani continues:

> *I was recently in DC, and I got the chance to meet Chuck Sams, the first Native man to direct the Park Service. And he's serving under Deb Haaland, the first native Secretary of the Interior. And I couldn't be more proud of him. But he's just a guy. He puts on his pants one leg at a time. He's got family, and people that he's responsible to. He's got a community, just like me. You don't have*

to be a hero. You just have to be accountable. There's no need to put him, or anyone else doing the work, on a pedestal. Because the only person I owe that to is God Almighty.

So I'm not going to deify these institutions or people like they're untouchable. They're just people too. The only difference between them and me is chronology and life experience.

God alone provides for us all. That knowledge helps. Understanding that the same God provides daily bread for us all, helps me engage with these institutions. It gives a sense of equality under God.

When you understand that God will take care of it, and that the promises of God are true, you find the confidence to believe you'll see the goodness of the Lord, here and now, while we're still in the land of the living. That gives you a certain level of detachment that helps continuing in the work, and navigating through these institutions and their tensions.

Even with a deep sense of groundedness and humility, we need to continue deliberately cultivating and nurturing our inner life. We need to commit to disciplines of self-care. Burning out along the way to repair serves no one's interests. Imani is just as committed to the walk of self-sustenance as she is to truth telling.

To keep that faith going, you have to spend intentional time in your deep emotions, developing that integrity. I spend a lot of time in prayer, wrestling with the question of who God is for me. I spend time in research, learning how white supremacy manifests, learning how patriarchy manifests. Part of my obligation in response to that learning is to heal myself. I will not compromise on that. I won't be one of those people who offers up their body to gears of the system just to keep them grinding. I'm not going to work myself to exhaustion.

And I pick my battles. I'm not going to argue with people who don't believe I'm human. I'm not going to be the one woman in the room who gets asked to take the minutes. I won't do it. I'm clear about my boundaries.

Imani continued, offering how faith helps her put the long-haul nature of this struggle in perspective:

You need to hold onto the fact that we're in a protracted struggle. I once learned how native communities kept this idea of being part of fourteen generations: the seven generations that went before you, the ones who made the sacrifices, and put in the work, and the seven generations that come after you, the ones who will be impacted by the choices and decisions you make. That's the perspective we need to hold onto. I learned this as a result of the Piscataway people in Maryland, but that ideology is pervasive amongst several groups.

In a contemporary movement, like reparations, you might not get it done, but your actions could reverberate down seven generations. So I do that it's my job to do as much as I can, while I can, and trust that the weight of it may be felt in subsequent generations.

And again, there's that church background. We're told we struggle not against flesh and blood, but against powers and principalities of spiritual wickedness in high places. And I've seen that. I've seen people controlled by evil energy. I've seen people possessed by the devil. White supremacy is only one example of what that looks like.

So we need to see ourselves, and our struggles, fitting into this grand melodrama of good vs. evil. Our job is to fight one small battle at a time. To lay one brick at a time in a wall of protection that gets built generation by generation.

Drawing out the connection between that grand arc of God's justice, and the day by day grind of making repair in our local communities and church committees can be tough. It takes a certain leap of faith to believe they're part of the same picture. Imani says it's helpful to focus on the specifics:

> *You have to hold that big vision, and then focus on the little stuff in front of you. Because the work, that fight, happens in very small victories. One of my first experiences in organizing was a voter registration drive out of my church in Davidson County when I was in eighth grade. And it was taking down one person's name at a time. Getting one signature, on one card. Until we got the job done.*
>
> *You have to take that grand vision of good vs. evil, and make it really, really practical. You need to talk about measurable goals, and benchmarks, while still keeping the overall strategy in mind.*
>
> *You know, two days ago I was driving, and I saw a family panhandling on the side of this very busy road, out in this summer heat. And what were they asking for? Not prayers. Bread, and shelter. But also there's policy. We have to ask how they got there. What's going on that risking your life, and your family's life on the side of the road is the best option you've got? We have to ask that big picture question, while also helping with their immediate needs right now, at this moment.*

For some, your spiritual grounding may come by way of deep moral conviction: a recognition and understanding that reparation is precisely the work that Jesus has called us toward, the work of the Gospels. Robinson describes it this way:

> *To me it's the Great Commandment to love one another, to love my neighbor as myself. And not just love my neighbor, but*

to better understand my neighbor, this discovery has to happen. The need to know about my neighbor. The need to be interested in what has made them who they are, get that connection to them, and hopefully have some empathy for their trials and tribulations as I would hope they would have for mine.

For me, the faith connection was the desire to help generate some level of peace, knowledge, and reconciliation. Because until we get to that point, we're just going to be knocking heads one way or another.

And Baxter lays it out this way:

In scripture Jesus says, if you come to make your offering, and you remember you have something against your brother, then leave your offering behind, and go and make things right, and then come back.

Reparations is all about that. It's all about trying to right injustices and wrongs that happened in the past. If we, as the church, can't do that, I don't expect anybody else to do it.

Reparations means looking at past injustices, learning how we can grow from them, and learning how we can make the people we've injured whole, so we can all continue on in our path. That, in my opinion, is the work of forgiveness. That's what discipleship is all about. Being forgiven for what you've done wrong, and forgiving others when they do wrong to you.

The work that we're doing is a witness to the world that, yes, the church gets it wrong sometimes, but we're going to keep plugging away to get it right.

4. Humility and a Growth Mindset

You will get this wrong. You will make mistakes along the way. You will get used to the taste of humble pie. If you begin the work of reparations with the hope that you can get all the details just right, or that your walk will be impeccable, you are setting yourself up for disappointment, resignation and resentment. And yet, we still must strive to do the work well. So begin with an attitude of humility, and approach the work with a growth mindset. Take joy in the learning. Be grateful that when you make a misstep, and it's pointed out to you, you now have an opportunity to not make that same mistake again. Maggiano and Memorial Church have named this kind of humility as a core principle of their reparations work:

> We have to keep acknowledging that we don't know how to do this. Nobody knows how to do this. So we're going to make mistakes. And when we make mistakes, all we can do is apologize, and seek to do better the next time.
>
> That's been a learning for me in leadership, from long before I came to Memorial, that someone has to be the person who doesn't need to take credit for the work, and someone has to be the person who's willing to acknowledge when things have gone bad and try and make them better.
>
> That's how I lead at Memorial, and how I model leadership for the congregation. And that has really informed our reparations work.

Often, this kind of humility requires us to relinquish a cherished dream or idea, in order to stay true to the core commitments and relationships we've created along the way. This is tough, because we get attached to our bright ideas, even when it becomes clear they aren't as bright as we thought. Maggiano led his congregation through relinquishing one such dream.

> We had a powerful relationship with this church, St. Catherine's. And since the pandemic started, they had been operating without a clergy person. There were financial considerations on their

end. I had this idea. We were in a position to hire an associate rector here. I thought, what if they served here during the week, doing pastoral stuff, and on Sunday's they'd be at St. Catherine's to preach and lead worship? And we'd pay for it all. That way they'd have a clergy person on Sundays. And I went through all the planning with our leaders and vestry [the Episcopal equivalent of a church board of directors] *and it was all in place, and then I went to talk to St. Catherine's leaders, to tell them what we were planning.*
And they said no.

And I said, "Why not?" Because I had gotten really excited. We talked through it, and considered three or four different ways to do it. Finally, Eileen Bridge Law, who's the senior board member there said, "This church is not ready. It's not ready to be led by a white church."

And at that moment, I could have just withdrawn and quit.

For Maggiano, and Memorial Church, this was a crucial inflection point. When our best and brightest ideas meet rejection, and especially when it comes from the people we are trying to do right by, it is very tempting to throw up our hands, shout "Well if you don't want our help … ," and walk away. I can all but guarantee this will happen for you at some point along your path toward making reparation. When this happened, we get to choose: will we cling to our own cherished plans, or we will let them go, and hold fast instead to that core commitment of repairing relationship? Memorial chose relationship.

I said to myself, "No, you have to listen." And as I listened I learned that St. Catherine's, even though they were founded in the eighteen nineties, they didn't become their own church until the nineteen seventies.

Resources for Perseverance 165

They had always been a mission of a white congregation. And so you have people in this church who are still on vestry, who remember that long fight for independence, and don't want to see that go back the other way, not in their lifetimes.

That was extremely humbling for me to have, first to realize how blind I had been, but second, to go back to our vestry and say, "we're not pursuing this."

Because they were super excited about it too, and would have felt really great. And so instead we committed to support them when they need help, whether it's financially, or doing services together, whatever they need, but only what they ask for. And both sides know Memorial could do more. But they want to do it themselves. And that may mean their church doesn't survive in the way I think it should. But it's not my church. It's not my community. And just because we've decided in the last two years to finally care about something we've been messing up for a hundred and fifty years, doesn't give us the right to step in and take it all over.

There's been a couple other times where I've messed up parts of that relationship. They've been harmed so much that there's just not a lot of trust. Once I started putting trust with them before anything else, the relationship improved. And that trust begins with being clear that I don't have the right to decide how this should work for them.

Walking in trust can be tough. Moving forward with integrity can be humbling. I know this personally. But I also want you to hear Maggiano's witness that "the relationship improved." I won't make you the naive promise that everything will be fine, or that everyone will be happy with the end result. Your reparations process will get rough. There's a good chance things will get worse before they get better.

Remember the process of reparations speaks to healing and health. Sometimes the path toward health sucks. Debriding and disinfecting old wounds hurts. Medicine tastes bad. Exercising is a chore. As I write these words, I sit in a waiting room, with a Ziplock bag of carrots and cherry tomatoes in my pocket, across from a snack table overflowing with free chocolate chip *cookies*. Choosing the vegetables is, at best, *disappointing*.

And yet, when we stick with them, the disciplines of health bring their rewards: energy, clarity, vitality, strength, wholeness and perhaps most *importantly*, more and better time spent in loving fellowship. Your reparations work will be the same. Build your resources for perseverance from the get-go, so you won't give up before you fruits of your effort emerge.

CHAPTER

11

A Principled Critique

D r. Catherine Meeks is the Executive Director of the Absalom Jones Center for Racial Healing. She's been at the work of racial justice for more than fifty years. I was privileged to sit with her on a panel discussion of reparations. She offered a critique, and a warning, regarding the possibility of reparations that I believe anyone taking on this work must hear. For that reason, I'm presenting our conversation uncut and in its entirety.

**I hear a lot of bad faith critiques of reparations,
but it struck me that you have a very principled criticism.
Could you share that perspective?**

I have a lot of concerns about reparations. It's like "reconciliation," and "love," and "community." We just throw words around and they don't mean anything; and the behaviors associated with them don't end up meaning anything, either.

You want to repair this chasm between the races. You're going to go out to find folks whose ancestors were enslaved and give them money. How are you going to decide what you need to give to them? Who gave you the capacity to value what was lost?

You get into so many questions you can't answer that it becomes a joke. You give me two thousand dollars because my great grandfather helped to build Georgetown University, or you let my kids go to college for free, because somebody was a slave. But what about creating a world where my kids could have had what they needed, because I could have made the money to pay for them to go to college? What about equity? In terms of education, housing and all the rest? Where do we stand on those issues in relation to the people, you're giving this money?

The idea of giving money to compensate for something in the past is the biggest problem I have with it. You can write the check, and now you don't have to worry about the twenty-first century deficits in equity you're still creating, because you paid the check, and you can tell yourself it's done now. And you haven't done anything. I get so mad with what Virginia Theological Seminary (VTS) is doing.

Their reparation initiative?

Yes. I'm so aggravated with them for making such a big to-do, when they haven't really done anything much about significant systemic change. Since they started, they've graduated two or three classes of students, whose lives haven't been touched in any way by the project. And their students who are going out to become religious leaders need to be learning more about how to address oppression and I cannot see how their current plan for reparations teaches them anything.

But they're doing this thing regarding reparations, finding these descendants of slaves, and inviting them to lunch, and giving them a little bit of a check. And it doesn't impact a single solitary person that's graduating. It doesn't help anybody go out and be a better priest, a priest that knows how to deal with injustice in a different way which is so needed.

I asked them: "How is this impacting your students? How are you making them people who won't continue putting energy into the systems that caused the harms that you say need reparation in the first place?"

Let's have a real conversation. Let's be serious about deconstructing these old ways of being and replacing them with something new that's enlivening. I'm not interested in anyone trying to pay me for what happened to my great grandfather. I want my great grandchildren not to have to live in the environment that my great grandfather had to live in, or that my children have to live in. I want them not to be afraid to live in this country because of its inequities and the bad ways in which we are perceived.

I know that's a big piece to work on. But if we're not willing to engage that work, then writing a check becomes an irrelevancy. Because you can't pay your way out of this, you have to live your way out of it. White people can't get done with slavery by writing a few checks to a few folks who who's relatives were enslaved, passing out checks without taking substantive steps to dismantle systemic racism will keep on reinforcing racism, and all of the practices that go with it.

Giving up the money becomes counterproductive in the long run, because now you think it's settled the issue. VTS found a handful of descendants of enslaved persons who worked there to give checks. They set aside a million dollars, and then they took the interest from it, which turned out not to be that much money, and used that to cut some people a few checks. When I asked about the impact of what VTS is doing I was given the following example. There was one Black man who's a descendant of somebody who was an enslaved worker at VTS, who now comes to lunch at the cafeteria sometimes, and eats with a few of the students. I was startled by that being

given as example of the way in which their program is having an impact upon their students. I cannot see how this simple occasional act of a few white people eating lunch with an
elderly Black man can be seen as a pathway to the transformation of systemic racism when it is not joined with other intentional efforts to do so. And the attention around that this effort
is gaining worries me. Because they made a big public splash
about the one million dollars being set aside without making it
clear that the plan was to use the interest which is amounting
to a far lesser amount. And now you've got many others running around thinking that they should all be doing what VTS
is doing, like that's the answer. But what VTS is doing isn't
getting at the crucial work of destabilizing systemic racism in
the way that will eventually result in a better chance at a life
without oppression.

I've heard some of the descendants refused the money,
because they were asking: "How are you going to pay me for
this? For the damage that's been done? I'm not going to let you
pay off your guilt with a check."

**That is my biggest anxiety around this work: that the church
will take it as a kind of wergild, where we say, "We paid it.
We're done. We don't want to hear about it." At the same
time, I do think there's a question of fair accounting. The
church, the Episcopal Church in particular, has amassed a
great deal of wealth that it plundered, in one way or another,
from the Black community. If we undertake the process of
building equity in a serious way, as you described, what do
you think should happen with those unjustly hoarded riches?**

It is important for some money to be engaged here. But the
question is, how do you engage it?

The physical church does have plenty of money. We like to sing our poor song, but we've got plenty of money when we decide we want to use it. That money should be invested in helping to create equitable and brave spaces. That money should go into Black communities, to help people to do work on developing stabilizing strategies in the community as a whole. In our Black communities, and particularly in the ones that are poor, there's so many resources lacking.

What if the church took on alleviating the squalor in poor communities by working on affordable housing? What if we put our money together with the United States government's housing money to eliminate poor quality housing? Because it is disproportionately Black and brown people getting pushed into projects that stack in a whole bunch of people together, and create hard, bad, places to live. We could focus on lack of good housing, or homelessness.

Or what if we wanted to focus on education? We could go to communities, with schools that were struggling, and we would use our resources, and our money, and our bodies, to help speak to deficits that exist in this community and help. Sometimes they do need money. Sometimes they need people.

Or we could focus on health. Nutrition is a serious problem. We've got these sprawling food deserts. We could do something about that. If VTS had gone on a campaign and said, "Okay, we raised one million dollars for reparations. We're going to find one of the poor Black areas of our city, and we're going to build a grocery store, and we're going to put in the money to make sure it stays open, so everyone can have access to it," I would've been much happier. Because now, you've started to destabilize some of that negative energy. You start putting something into the community that's got some potential to provide transformation.

Or we could build a community center, or focus on almost any question of environmental justice, because those are all racialized too. There are so many communal issues we could focus on, where the money would be very useful, and it would benefit everybody.

But I'm totally opposed to giving any single person any money. If you give me a check and I go buy three more handbags that I didn't need in the first place, and you feel really good about yourself, what does it do for anybody?

VTS can try to pick out the fifteen folks they say are descended from people who worked in various places there as enslaved persons, but if you give those fifteen people the money, then they'll go across town to the grocery store, outside the community, and spend until their money runs out. And then that's it. So I think that individual piece is a big mistake.

If you invest in the community, then everyone benefits. If you want to really talk about reparations, it ought to be about communities and not individuals.

But I know it's not a popular opinion. I've had to spend a lot of time thinking about why this conversation on reparations troubles me so much. We say, "Let the white folks write checks." Now they feel like they're sacrificing something. But they're not really sacrificing. There's no follow through.

VTS put aside a million dollars and other entities have done similar acts, and then they draw interest off it for the distributions to individuals or to give scholarships. And they get bushel baskets of great publicity from it. But what have they actually done? What's the annual interest on a million dollars? A few thousand dollars, maybe twenty-five thousand, and that is distributed with the long term effect being quite minimal.

That sounds about right.

It's not much. And when I approached them on behalf of the Center for Racial Healing, and asked: "Can we partner with you on this? You've got this money, let's do something good with it." They answered, "Well, it's not actually going to be that much money." And they had the plan to focus on individuals in place already.

So there's nothing substantial happening there. But "reparations" has become such a buzzword around the church, and VTS and others who have similar plans to give money to enslaved persons descendants are becoming a model as I said before and it worries me that we are using these models that are not inclusive enough to really create the type of change necessary. to actually help dismantle systemic racism. So I want to walk back to a conversation about equity, deconstruction of systemic oppression, and reconstruction of something that speaks to the long term. I want little Black and brown kids to have communities that are safe and healthy, where they can get a decent education and don't have to worry about being shot down in the street like a dog.

That's my idea of what good reparations should be. It should be about structural change. It should be about creating a new kind of environment, a new world where it's safe to be a Black person in the United States of America, which it isn't at the moment. If your ideas about repairing the breach don't cover some of that then it feels to me like you just didn't think it through.

I saw that in New York they just gave out a whole bunch of scholarships. I think it's great to give kids scholarships to go to college. I have no problem with that, but quit making that sound like you just fixed everything. You gave twenty scholarships to twenty Black kids. That's marvelous. But what about the little kids sitting on the stoop who can barely read and write, and their school is pitiful? Go ahead and give the scholarships. But don't give the scholarships thinking that's the end of the story, because that's just one piece of the puzzle. If you care about Black kids going to college, you need to care what kind of eight grade they have, too. And you need to care about what kind of third grade they have, because that's the base. Did you know the prisons project how many new beds they can add in future years based on how many kids are failing third grade right now? They're betting on the failure of our Black kids. Reparations ought to be speaking to that kind of thing, and it isn't right now. Now it's just about giving individual people money.

I don't know who thought of that idea. But it never seemed like a good idea to me. We choose the easy way out by choosing to address individuals rather than systems. In the church people want to stay around individualizing racism. They'll say it doesn't exist because I'm not a racist, or that because I'm progressive everything's okay, or that because I'm okay with everybody there isn't a problem.

And it is important for individuals to claim their stuff. But you can't deny the systems And this reparations conversation isn't dealing with systemic racism. It's characterized as doing that. but it's basically very individualistic. You're trying to choose individuals and compensate them individually. You're not speaking to the bigger issue of systemic racism at all.

You mentioned the trend of people, and I imagine it's especially my people, white people, individualizing the issue: thinking "because I'm not racist, in a personal sense, there isn't a problem." It seems like part of the work of The Center

for Racial Healing is helping people to get committed and tackle systemic racism. What have you found effective in getting people past that individualistic framework?

It's been an uphill climb. This is our fifth year now of doing this work. A lot of it was about getting folks to wake up, period. And then once you wake up, what do you do? We have a whole section of the Center called the Barbara Harris Justice Project that looks at mass incarceration, the death penalty, health inequities, environmental justice and immigration.

We want to say to people that once you wake up to your individual stuff, and you think you've become pretty progressive, and you know the lay of the land, then there's this work out there for you to go and do. Now you know and here are areas of work you can connect to. And we'll offer resources to help you do it. You can also find your own way very easily too. There's plenty to do, and lots of information about how to do it.

But you don't get to sit down and just be conscious. You get to take your consciousness, and walk it outside to engage with the world. And we have gotten responses from churches that have said: "Okay, we need to stop just offering book studies, and actually go out and do something."

The other thing we've tried to do is wake people up to the fact that racial healing is a process of spiritual formation. You have to do it until you die. There's no point at which you get to lean back, cross your arms and say: "Okay, that's it. I did it. I've arrived."

We try to keep people from going back to sleep. We try to keep them going down the road, and practicing whatever racial healing work they're up to, because every day God's calling you to go a little deeper, to be a little braver, to go a little further. There's always the frontier ahead.

I'm seeing some people and some churches step up to that idea. Sometimes that shows up as them trying to launch their own dismantling-racism-curriculum or racial justice program. So they're globalizing, instead of partnering with the people already doing work in their neighborhoods. That is something we need to work on. But the idea of always pushing forward, to build something better, that idea's taking hold, a little bit.

And we keep preaching that that's the goal. It's not that you get to check some box off and be comfortable. The more you wake up, the more God can expect of you.

Some days I wish I didn't know anything. Because, if I didn't, I could just have my life. But I know all this stuff, and I see all this stuff, all these injustices, and I can't leave it alone.

Our constant mantra is that there is no camping and resting, that it is all about vigilance and saying yes to whatever God puts in your path.

Coming back to your question, I'm not going to tell you what to do. Because it's God who's calling you to do something. And I'm not in the business of playing God for other folks. I don't know specifically what it is you're supposed to be doing.

What I do know, for absolute fact, is that God is calling you to do something. Your job is to figure out what that is. Now, if we can be helpful in figuring that out, we want to help. That's what all our classes are about. That's what all our writing is about. That's what our consulting is about. But you have to do the work yourself.

After George Floyd was killed, I had so many people contacting me asking, "What should I do?" My best answer was: "Sit down, stand still, find out what God wants you to do, because I have no clue." How are you asking me what you need to be doing? It's like you calling me up at five o'clock, saying what should I cook for supper? I don't know what you have in your kitchen. I don't know your nutritional needs. I don't know what you want to eat. You have to figure that out.

It's the same thing with this work. You have to find the courage to figure it out for yourself. We get the whole thing is such a mess because we're looking for prescriptions. We want someone to tell us "just do this one thing, and everything will be fine."

That's part of my issue with reparations. People are looking for a way to do social justice quickly. They're thinking: "Tell us to do reparations. That's easy. We can raise some money. We can pay off these debts."

But if you're not changing structures, five generations from now Black folks will be far worse off than they were when you did whatever little reparations thing it was that you did. If we're really looking to repair, we need to think about how to create a world where these injuries stop happening.

You know Peter, my brother, my twelve-year-old brother, died because he couldn't get medical care in a white hospital in Arkansas. My father lived his whole life with PTSD because he lost my twelve-year-old brother and couldn't do anything about it. My father died when I was sixteen, but that was just a belated announcement. He'd already died alongside my little brother.

So somebody comes along and says, "We want to give you reparations now." What are you going to give to us to compensate for his life? How are you going to make any legitimate compensation to him, to me, or to our family? You give us all the money on the planet, and it still won't be enough.

But here's what you could do. You could do something about the way hospitals are set up. You could do something about the way medical care is done. You could do something about helping to elect officials that care about people, so that they don't circumvent Medicaid coming to the poor folks. You could create a new medical system, so that in the future, no child will ever die because his skin is Black or because he's poor.

That's a better goal. That's how people of faith should be thinking. Because there is no compensation for the wounds.

I want to create a world where kids can be seen for who they really are rather than on the basis of somebody's projections. That's going to take a long time. It's not going to happen in my lifetime. But It's never going to happen if we don't start down a different path. The Episcopal Church could be leading that effort. We could be doing something so phenomenal and we're just missing the chance. There's so much we could do. It's not as glamorous or eye-catching as handing out checks. But it's more significant.

We're going to have to turn a bunch of stuff upside down, and get rid of it, and start something new, and it's going to be revolutionary. And I don't think most people have got the stomach for it. So it's easier to do all this band-aid stuff, because you can feel pretty good about it, and it keeps you from having to deal with that real need to reconstruct the system.

We don't want to do that. We want things to pretty much rock along. We want to tweak it. We want to clean it up, so we can feel better about it. We don't care much if it changes, as long as we can feel better about it.

Do you remember what I said on that Saturday, at the panel discussion? I said you need to think about how you feel, personally, about poor people. You're up here having a big conversation about reparations that you want some white person to take care of so they don't have to feel guilty. But you're cursing the person living under the bridge, or the person you see at the stop light who's asking you for a dollar for dinner. For me, that's another place where Christians have to interrogate themselves. What is my attitude toward folks who don't have what they need? How do I want to serve them and help them to be engaged? I need to answer that for myself as well when I'm thinking about all of this stuff, because it's all the same piece of fabric.

The work you're describing is long haul work, and requires a deep, internal interrogation. It strikes me that a lot of institutions, and individuals fall by the wayside when we realize that the kind of quick solutions you were describing won't be sufficient. We give up when we see, as you were saying, that this is a lifelong commitment, and the work of many generations. But you've been at this a good while. And while I respect your position that you can't tell anyone else what they should be doing, I also believe there's value in learning from the experience of seasoned veterans. So, may I ask, what sustains you in the work?

Well, some of it's just stubbornness. But a lot of it is getting clarity about what my call is. It's taken me a long time to be willing to engage in this conversation at all. I always knew, from way back in the seventies when we started the reparations conversation, that I didn't agree with what folks were saying. But I didn't know why. So it's taken me these forty years to get it straight in my head: why am I so troubled by that?

But now I can say, I'm troubled because it's just short sighted. I've become really pretty radical myself when it comes to economics. We have let capitalism run away with us. We're letting it kill us. We very, very badly need to get a grip on that. I've come to understand how much we don't like poor people. And I come from poor people. So at this point I feel called to live on the margins.

Getting clarity about where I'm situated, and who I'm to be, and what I'm supposed to be, and what I'm supposed to say in this whole conversation, has sustained me. It teaches me what I should be doing at each moment.

I don't see myself out here with a flag, rushing down the highway to overturn the government. But I do believe that it's my job to say that until we're willing to turn over the systems, and deconstruct them, and reconstruct them, with everybody's welfare in mind, we're not going to get anywhere. Having that clarity of what you want to say, and finding the courage to say it, can sustain you through a lot.

And then there's faith. I believe God is more interested in equity than inequity. I believe God is very disturbed by the way we have created hierarchies of value for human beings, and constructed our reality on those hierarchies. God is not happy with that. And anybody who's trying to be decent shouldn't be happy with it, either.

Getting all that straight, getting ingrained in my psyche helps me. Because I've been on this path, and talking about this, for fifty years. That's a long, long time. And just to witness the hatred toward black people, and the violence of the police against us, is really hard. There's a lot of rage that comes from living in a Black body in a world that's not interested in people in Black bodies.

But I get up every morning determined to stay focused and stay with it. Because for me that's it. That's my answer to how to live in this messed up world. I have to stay focused on what I know I'm called to do. I have to trust I am making a difference, by being willing to let my voice be courageous and let it be used in this way.

I'm not going to see most of the difference it will make. But I trust in the process, that if we keep on destabilizing this stuff long enough, one of these days it'll break. I really believe that.

I also have a community of people that sustains me: friends, family, professional colleagues, church people. I'm part of the society of Saint Anna the Prophet. We are thirty five women committed to praying for each other, and praying together, and we have vows to live with balance, creativity and simplicity. I have support systems that help sustain me.

And the last thing is, I've spent a lot of money on psycho-therapy and spiritual direction.

Is it okay if I tell you I've spent a lot of money on both of those too?

They do help when we're trying to get whole. And I guess that comes back to my main point. We've got to deeply interrogate ourselves to find a way out of this mess. There are no quick solutions. And I think reparations, the way people are talking about it, is an attempt to find a quick solution.

Conclusion

The Necessity and Insufficiency
of Financial Reparations

One insight I hope we've all learned along this way. Financial reparations are not a cure-all. We could write a check for all the money in the world, and still not remedy the troubles of white supremacy. And yet, the money matters, and must be accounted for. As we try to move toward making reparations, we must come to clearly understand financial reparations as both *necessary* and *insufficient* remedy for the injuries of white supremacy.

Economists, logicians and computer scientists use the language of necessity and sufficiency when evaluating solutions to a specific problem. A necessary solution is one that must be in place to solve that problem. If you're thirsty, water is a necessary solution. Maybe you drink it from the tap, maybe you like it bottled, or maybe get it in fruit juice or milk. But there's no way to get from thirsty to not-thirsty except water: water is a necessary solution for thirst.

A sufficient solution is one that, on its own, with no other remedy or assistance, can solve the problem at hand. If you're thirsty simply because it's hot out and you've been running, drinking a glass of water will get the job done. It is a necessary and sufficient solution. But if the cause of your thirst is deeper, more severe, water alone might not cut it.

Twenty years ago, I got sick with cholera. It was, apparently, a mild case. I still wouldn't wish it on anyone. The great danger of cholera is dehydration. When cholera kills, that's how it happens. So, you need water to survive cholera, and lots of it. Water is a necessary solution for the problem. But it isn't sufficient. The massive and rapid dehydration of cholera also strips your body of salt and other necessary electrolytes. Those must be replenished too. In my case, that involved forcing down a mixture of water, salt, lime juice and sugar in such great quantities that I came to loathe the stuff.

In severe cases, patients will require antibiotics, as well. The still raging infection will drain water and electrolytes from your body faster than any IV can keep up. The infection must be destroyed before health and wholeness can replace dehydration and thirst. Where cholera is concerned, water is an always necessary, but sometimes insufficient, remedy.

It's important, as we consider the topic of reparations, that we come to understand financial reparations as a necessary, but insufficient, remedy for white supremacy in the church. That is to say, there is no path to overcoming white supremacy that does not involve financial reparations. And, at the same time, financial reparations alone will not free us from white supremacy's clutches.

If we fail to accept the necessity of financial reparations, then in all likelihood, we (white people) are chasing after fantasies of racial reconciliation without genuine sacrifice. We are hoping to somehow absolve ourselves for the sin of anti-Black racism, while keeping the benefit we receive from it. And that is impossible.

On the other hand, If we do not reckon with the insufficiency of reparations, then in all likelihood we (again, white people) are looking for a quick fix: a check we can write so we can pat ourselves on the back, say we've done enough, and never talk about it again. If we are serious about accomplishing the work of racial justice we must have both the necessity and the insufficiency of financial reparations fixed clearly in our minds.

The Necessity of Reparations

The necessity of financial reparations is a matter of both practical and spiritual concern.

Most white folks (including myself) fail to understand the lived financial impact of white supremacy on Black and brown folk. Several factors contribute to sabotaging our comprehension.

First, American culture, and white American culture in particular, has a peculiar taboo against openly discussing our finances and wealth, confounding our efforts to clearly perceive and understand economic inequities.

As a pastor, I've walked many couples through the process of pre-marital counseling. My goals for these sessions are modest: I try to make sure they can communicate and negotiate effectively around time, money, family and sex, these being, in my observation, the places most couples hit rough patches. Our session on money is consistently the most difficult. When it comes time to talk about finances, couples suddenly grow quiet. Oftentimes I learn they haven't ever spoken with one another about their assets, debts and spending habits.

Surprisingly, these sessions are almost always more difficult than our conversations around sex. In those sessions, I'll tell couples that I don't want to hear particulars, I just need to know whether they're able to communicate with one another about their sex lives. And despite that disclaimer, they frequently share, unsolicited, far more detail than I requested or felt comfortable hearing.

But getting couples to discuss their finances is like pulling teeth. In talking with other pastors, I've learned this pattern is not uncommon. Despite the conflicted prudish prurience of society, our taboo against discussing personal finances runs far deeper and stronger than that against discussing sex. Not being a historian, or sociologist, I can't say definitively how or why this taboo emerged, but I will venture a guess.

We pride ourselves on being an egalitarian nation. Any level of serious research reveals the fantasy of this notion. Even leaving aside academic investigation, if you pick a given street corner of any city in this country, choose one direction, and walk that way for three miles with your eyes open, you will see the lie of our egalitarian dreams, as you pass from poverty to wealth and back again.

Our taboo against discussing wealth guards that fantasy. When we refuse to honestly acknowledge and account for what we each have (or don't), we fall into the pretense that we all belong to some amorphous, poorly defined middle class. It becomes impossible to identify, much less address, the inequities among us. And we fail to see the patterns of race within those inequities.

For this very reason in recent years many women and people of color have pushed businesses and nonprofits to publish salary bands for job offerings, and to encourage a culture of openness around what different employees in the same workplace are paid. In order to recognize and understand the deep racial inequities that surround us we must normalize talking openly, frankly and honestly about our own finances and wealth. We can begin by asking ourselves why we are reticent or embarrassed to openly discuss our income and wealth? What are we trying to hide?

For we who call ourselves Christians, this is a matter of spiritual formation. Jesus talks more about the Kingdom of God than anything else, but money, and what we do with it, comes in a close second. And in his teaching, these two topics are closely intertwined. So how can we possibly hope to follow him as disciples, if we are unwilling to even use the principal language of his teaching?

To make matters worse, we stigmatize poverty and financial struggle, so that those most directly impacted by racialized financial inequities are often deeply reluctant to speak about the lived reality of economic hardships. And to be clear, this is not their fault. It is the fault of we who benefit from this unjust system. Consciously or otherwise, we have created, reinforced and participated in a culture of shaming the poor. We shame them into silence. And their silence protects our comfort. It protects us from being confronted with personal, human-level consequences of racialized economic inequity. In general we won't hear about it from people we know personally, so we are free to imagine the problem of racialized poverty in the abstract. We can think of it as something that exists "out there," rather than something that impacts people in our orbit. This makes it easier to bear, or to ignore.

The Episcopal Church has a particular responsibility in creating this culture of shaming the poor. We have been, and in many ways continue to be one of the most deeply classist Christian denominations in this country. For much of our history, we took pride in being the destination church of the aspirationally middle and upper class. We attempted to baptize classism and poverty-shaming as a kind of spiritual and theological discipline. When poverty is racialized, as it is in this country, that means an attempt to baptize racism as well.

We must unmake, and unlearn, this habit of spiritual and theological stigmatization. We can begin by noting, and questioning, any thought or belief in ourselves that suggests wealth is a product of virtue or hard-work.

Again, this is a matter of spiritual formation. Jesus was never queasy naming the question of who is impoverished, and who is enriched. And far from shaming the poor, he seems much more inclined to point an accusatory finger at the wealthy. These are teachings we shy away from. We smile politely as we hear Christ declare "Blessed are the poor," but I've yet to hear a preacher who made Jesus's rebuke: "Woe to you who are rich," the central verse of their sermon. Maybe all we preachers should all try it, as a necessary corrective away from the sanctified poverty-shaming our church has embraced.

Given that our taboo against money talk and our stigmatization of poverty sabotage any chance for honest discourse racial economic inequality, our only hope for really comprehending the truth of things would be from direct experience. But here again, we are hamstrung. Because that kind of experience could come only in the context of a trusting relationship. It would mean being invited to walk with people of color in their lives and homes. The chances for this are vanishingly small. A much-publicized 2014 study from the Public Religion Research Institute found that three-quarters of white Americans don't have a single Black friend, and a majority of those that do only have one. We remain deeply and profoundly segregated. If we're honest, we (white people) must acknowledge that we know almost nothing of Black people, or the Black community in this country.

I'm hesitant to offer a prescription on that point. The last thing Black people need is a bunch of white folk like me running around trying to collect Black friends to bump up our numbers. But we should at least acknowledge that, assuming love requires learning, acquaintance, and contact, then we are failing at our Savior's command to "love your neighbor as yourself."

In the absence of honest conversation about wealth, in the absence of relationships and lived experience, all we have left is numbers and statistics. There is a galling one we should consider. According to the Federal Reserve's 2019 survey, the average wealth of a white family is nearly eight times that of a Black family's

I like numbers and statistics. I believe in them, when they're gathered with integrity. But numbers and statistics don't move our hearts. It's easy to generalize and abstractify these numbers. We might shake our heads sadly, before going on with our days, but we don't feel the human impact of that wealth gap.

I want to invite us all to try and feel it. I want to invite us to imagine what the lived cost of an eight-to-one wealth gap is. Imagine, feel, how that wealth gap impacts whether we'll be able to feed the people we love in the coming days, or whether we'll have a safe and healthy place to live next month, or if we can hope to pursue a dream without taking on a burden of crushing debt, or if we live with the knowledge that a single, small, stroke of bad luck could tear apart everything we've struggled a lifetime to build, because we have no cushion at all.

The cost of that wealth gap is measured in lifespan, health outcomes, education, public safety, the quality of neighborhood amenities and infrastructure, political agency, voting access and more. All of these things are deeply conditioned and determined by one's wealth. It shapes people's lives.

It's true that not all Black people face these struggles and afflictions. It is also true that there are white people who know these hardships intimately. But an eight-to-wealth gap means

that Black people contend with these troubles in vastly disproportionate numbers.

There is no path toward equity and well-being that does
not address that wealth gap directly. We try to avoid this conclusion hiding behind hollow platitudes that "rising tides raise
all boats" and "equal opportunities not equal outcomes." I suspect I know what we're hiding from. White Americans represent 61% of the population but own 80% of private wealth.
Black Americans represent 13% of the population but own
only 2.5% of private wealth.

There is a zero-sum equation at work. Closing the wealth
requires white America to surrender ill-gotten gains that we
have come to cherish. It demands sacrifice. Financial reparations are necessary.

The Insufficiency of Financial Reparations

The insufficiency of reparations is clear. The history of racist theft, abuse, rape and enslavement runs back four hundred
years. There is no paying for the blood. The debt is simply too
great. Offering financial compensation for that debt is not only
impossible, but galling,

In recalling her brother's death, Catherine Meeks asked
me: "what are you going to give us to compensate for his life?"

As she asked the question, I knew clearly that any answer I
could give would be insulting. I knew this personally. A member of my immediate family, beloved to me, was recently killed
by an act of police violence. He was Black. In some sense, the
circumstances of what happened don't matter. Our system
arranges for police to be in situations of violent confrontation
with Black people, and arms them for those confrontations.
From their inception in this country, arising out of slave patrols,

the unstated (and sometimes explicit) raison d'être of policing institutions has been to keep Black and brown in their place within the racialized hierarchy of this nation. So, when police kill Black people, it is an act of racist violence, by definition: the system works as intended. The systems and structures that were supposed to keep him safe and well, failed him at every turn, because the institutions of our society are designed to fail Black people. There is no paying for the lives that have been crushed through these failures. There is no paying for his life. As Meeks noted, all the money in the world still wouldn't be enough.

Even at the practical level, churches, dioceses and seminaries could divest themselves of all their assets, turn them over completely to the Black, Indigenous, and other brown communities they have wronged. They could do all that, and it wouldn't, on its own, change the covertly (or overtly) racist policies, practices and cultures of these institutions. Even without our endowments and church physical plants, and sprawling real estate, members of predominantly white institutions would still wield disproportionate social capital and influence. That old network of connections and soft power would still do its work, influencing investment plans, hiring practices and even legislative processes, to produce situations advantageous to whites and detrimental to everyone else. Financial reparations are insufficient.

Reparations are not a panacea or magic wand for the ills of white supremacy. But they are a necessary component in the work of racial justice precisely because they are difficult and messy, because they demand sacrifice and humility, because they require that we listen, learn from and follow the people our systems of dominance erase, because they force us to examine ourselves and to move with care and intention.

The choice facing us now is whether we will allow the ill-gotten gains of our church to drag us down into oblivion, or whether we will choose to release them and reach for the possibilities of what could come next. Though it may be insufficient, reparation is necessary. It's high past time we made it a reality.

Acknowledgments

Many thanks to everyone who contributed to this book in one way or another. I am grateful for all the members of the Reparations Task Force of the Episcopal Diocese of Washington, Susan Schulken, Anne Derse, The Rev. Dr. Gayle Fisher-Stewart, Dr. Enid LaGesse, The Rev. Melana Nelson-Amaker, The Rev. David Wacaster, Jonathan Nicholas, Cathy O'Donnell, Franklin Robinson, Rudy Logan, Hazel Monae, Allison Roulier, Emily Pearce, James Pearce and The Rev. Daryl Loban, with special thanks to Caroline Klam, who posed the question that launched our initiation. We've been blessed that our bishop, The Rt. Rev. Mariann Budde, Diocesan Council and our Standing Committee have supported and offered constructive criticism to this effort from the start.

The members of the Reparations Accountability Board: the Rev. Deacon Antonio Baxter, The Rev. Delonte Gholston, Karen May, Dr. Jocelyn Imani, Makia Green, Dr. Maurice Jackson, Natacia Knapper, Lindsay Ayers, Tom Brown, and The Rev. Dr. Julianne Robertson offered their time, effort and patient determination in keeping us honest and on track. We owe them a debt beyond words.

The Rev. Canon John Harmon identified and pushed on significant oversights in our process. I'm blessed he was willing to press the point.

I have been humbled by the courage of the Congregational Research Group of the Diocese of Washington, and their lay leaders, more than a dozen churches doing the difficult and uncomfortable work of investigating and sharing their own communities' histories with anti-Black racism.

Milton Brasher-Cunningham proposed the idea for this book, and championed it to Church Publishing once I agreed to take it on. Jennifer Amuzie encouraged me to make the effort, and suggested the structure of the final product.

I am immensely grateful to my seven colleagues in the work, Natacia, Lindsay, Gayle, Franklin, Jocelyn, Susan, and Antonio, who agreed to offer their experience, insights and perspectives in the interviews that became the core of this book, and especially to Dr. Catherine Meeks and Rev. Grey Maggiano, who hardly knew me at all but still offered to share their wisdom. Whatever virtue can be found in these pages belongs to these nine souls.

The editorial team at Church Publishing, especially Dana Knowles, Airié Stuart, Ryan Masteller, and Justin Hoffman, as well as copyeditor Jill Rupnow, gave this book a shot and carried it across the finish line. You wouldn't be reading it without them.

I owe everything that I am, and all I have to offer, to my wife Rondesia and my son Joshua, the loves of my life. I'm just glad they put up with me.

Praise and thanks to God, the repairer of all harms.